Sarah: Mother of Nations

TAMMI J. SCHNEIDER

SARAH

Mother of Nations

continuum
NEW YORK · LONDON

The Continuum International Publishing Group, 15 East 26th Street, New York, NY 10010

The Continuum International Publishing Group Ltd, The Tower Building, 11 York Road, London SE1 7NX

Cover art: Sarah by James J. Tissot, Jewish Museum, New York/SuperStock
Design: Corey Kent

Library of Congress Cataloging-in-Publication Data

Schneider, Tammi J. (Tammi Joy), 1962-
  Sarah : mother of nations / by Tammi J. Schneider.
    p. cm.
  Includes bibliographical references and index.
  ISBN 0-8264-1624-1 (hardcover) — ISBN 0-8264-1625-X (pbk.)
  1. Sarah (Biblical matriarch) 2. Bible. O.T. Genesis XI-XXII—Commentaries.
3. Bible. O.T. Genesis XI-XXII—Feminist criticism. I. Title.
  BS580.S25S36 2004
  222'.11092—dc22
                                      2004002404

Printed in the United States of America

04 05 06 07 08 09   10 9 8 7 6 5 4 3 2 1

To my family
FAROOQ, SARAH, *and* KALILAH

Contents

Acknowledgments ix

Abbreviations xi

Introduction 1

CHAPTER 1
The Beginning of the Story: Genesis 11 8

CHAPTER 2
Establishing Relationships: Genesis 12–13 24

CHAPTER 3
Changing Status: Genesis 14–17 42

CHAPTER 4
The Three Messengers' Announcement: Genesis 18–19 66

CHAPTER 5
The Evolving Family: Genesis 20–22 82

CHAPTER 6
Sarah's End: Genesis 23 111

Conclusions 124

Appendix: The New Testament 131

Bibliography 134

Index 138

Acknowledgments

This book would not have been possible without the help, advice, counsel, and support of a number of people, whom I wish to thank here.

I would like to thank Claremont Graduate University for their sabbatical policy, which provided me with two semester sabbatical leaves to work on this project. I am also fortunate to work with wonderful students, faculty, and staff from all the colleges in Claremont as well as the Claremont School of Theology. Their excitement, interest, and participation in my courses on Genesis and in my Genesis reading group provide insight, a sounding board for my ideas, and wonderful opportunities to engage the biblical text in different settings.

I am also very lucky to have some truly exceptional colleagues. Marvin Sweeney is not only one of the most gifted scholars I know but is also a truly wonderful person and my friend through everything. To have such a great mind asking me questions, discussing issues, and always supporting and pushing me is more than any friend or colleague could expect. Kristin de Troyer is my other Hebrew Bible colleague, and I consider it an honor to call her my friend. She has great insight into the different textual traditions, what they mean, and how they affect our interpretation of the Masoretic Text. Both my colleagues have a love of the Hebrew text and of life that keeps us discussing the Bible regardless of the late hour or how many bottles of wine we have consumed.

My luck continues by having been invited to teach in the Orange County Jewish Feminist Center for the last nine years. In preparation for our initial meeting I first seriously considered the role of Sarah in the Hebrew Bible. While discussing what I was preparing to teach for my class for them on "Women in the Bible," I mentioned to the Dean of the School of Religion, Karen Torjesen, that I was going to begin with Sarah because she is such a strong character. My colleague was confused since in her understanding and training Sarah is a weak character (for reasons related to the New Testament, discussed in the conclusions of this study). Thus began my interest in Sarah. My Orange County group has followed (or led me) in this journey, revisiting the character of Sarah numerous times, and yet they never seem to tire of our discussions of Sarah. They are so full of fresh ideas combined with such different and insightful life experiences that I cannot imagine being a scholar without such a wonderful group of muses.

Finally, I must thank my family. My love of anything related to a Sarah began with my adopted Aunt Sarah—may her memory be a blessing—whose joyous laughter I can still hear ringing in my ears. My mother has always assumed that there is nothing my siblings and I could not accomplish. Without my daughters, the world would not be as bright nor would I have the insight into what matters in life. My darling husband, Farooq Hamid, truly is my best friend. Without his support, help, sense of humor, and presence, this book simply could not have happened.

Abbreviations

ABD	*Anchor Bible Dictionary.* Edited by D. N. Freedman. 6 vols. New York, 1992
BDB	Brown, F., S. R. Driver, and C. A. Briggs. *A Hebrew and English Lexicon of the Old Testament.* Oxford, 1907
BHS	*Biblia Hebraica Stuttgartensia.* Edited by K. Elliger and W. Rudolph. 5th edition. Stuttgart, 1997
CAD	*Chicago Assyrian Dictionary = The Assyrian Dictionary of the Oriental Institute of the University of Chicago.* Edited by Martha T. Roth, A. Leo Oppenheim, Erica Reiner, et al. Chicago, 1956
CBQ	*Catholic Biblical Quarterly*
JPS	*Tanakh: A Translation of the Holy Scriptures according to the Traditional Hebrew Text,* Jewish Publication Society (JPS), 1917
JSOTSup	Journal for the Study of the Old Testament: Supplement Series
KJV	King James Version
LXX	Septuagint, Greek translation of the Hebrew Scriptures
MT	Masoretic Text
NASB	New American Standard Bible

NJPS   *Tanakh: A New Translation of the Holy Scriptures according to the Traditional Hebrew Text*, Jewish Publication Society (JPS), 1985
NKJV   New King James Version
NRSV   New Revised Standard Version
RSV   Revised Standard Version
SBL   Society of Biblical Literature
Vulgate   Latin Vulgate

Introduction

Sarah, the wife of Abraham and the mother of Isaac, is an important biblical character because of her role in the establishment of the people later called Israel.[1] The Hebrew Bible devotes more text to her than to most women, yet the stories about her are scattered and embedded in the larger narrative of Genesis in general and of Abraham in particular. As a result, though scholars have discussed her in recent years, they still have a rather scattered and diverse picture of her and her role in the text.

The image of Sarah has not always fared well in scholarship, which often views her in relationship to Hagar, her Egyptian slave, whom she treats harshly. As a result she appears as petty, indulgent, self-absorbed, and the oppressor of Hagar.[2] Others treat her as passive or in league with Abraham at his worst moments.[3] There are those who do not even consider her a good mother and describe her as overprotective.[4] Some also depict her as having no faith in the Israelite Deity.[5]

Other recent studies have examined Sarah in a slightly different light. According to some rabbinic texts, she is a symbol of hope and even a prophetess.[6] Tuebal goes so far as to claim that Sarah was a Mesopotamian priestess and the powerful one in the family.[7] Scholars are now examining the nuances in the role of Sarah's relationship with Abraham and Hagar and some of the larger issues in Genesis.[8]

These disparate views of Sarah emerge not just in one genre of biblical scholarship, but also in many different areas such as rhetorical criti-

1

cism, the more traditional source analysis, literary analyses, anthropolog-
ical approaches, and feminist critiques. The concept and character of
Sarah is of interest to many of the new approaches to the biblical text.
They have produced a wide range of ideas about who and what Sarah and
her role are in the text.

According to Jeansonne, "Until recently most modern interpreters of
the Book of Genesis have displayed patriarchal bias. Their commentaries
consider women chiefly in their function of supporting men and the por-
traits of women's lives are not examined seriously for their inherent significance."[9] My study evaluates the character of Sarah and her role in the
text of Genesis in order to understand how women function in the text,
how the biblical writers have constructed women's roles, and how this has
an impact on a modern reading of the Hebrew Bible. The approach will
be primarily literary. The stress is on the actual Hebrew and what the
words mean or could mean. Unless stated otherwise, I use my own translations because most versions try to make the text sound right for
English-speakers. I strive for a translation that best reflects the Hebrew
of the text. As soon as one translates, one begins to interpret the text; in
my examination I seek to excise some of the traditional interpretations
that have crept into the text already in the stage of translation work. This
study will also focus on other literary issues such as where a story begins
and ends, the portrayal of the various characters, and the role of the narrator, especially vis-à-vis the reader.

This study progresses on a number of premises. First, while there was
clearly a process by which the biblical text was constructed, that process
is impossible or almost impossible to discern. The process by which the
text was created is less important to this study than the final result of that
process. Furthermore, using a documentary approach to the text allows
scholars to avoid some of the more difficult questions about how various
elements of the text fit together as a unified story.[10] This book uses the
Masoretic Text (MT) as represented in the *Biblia Hebraica Stuttgartensia*
(*BHS*) as the representative text of the Hebrew Bible. Even though I will
use the MT, I recognize that it contains early textual variants and that
there is no "final" text of the Hebrew Bible.

Second, one of the oldest divisions of the text available to us is by the
Masoretes. The term "Masorah" (tradition) refers to the traditional Jewish rules governing the production of a handwritten copy of the biblical
text.[11] The Masoretes were scholars, possibly working as early as 500 C.E.,
whose job was to maintain the tradition that governed the production of

copies of the biblical text for liturgical or scholarly use.[12] The bulk of their scholarship concerned the consonants, vowels, and accent signs, but the Masoretic rules also governed the layout and division of the text.[13] As with the biblical text in general, manuscript codices differ in the Masoretic notes they include.[14] The claim may or may not be true that the Masoretic ben Asher family preserved the authentic tradition of the Holy Land and passed it along in unbroken line from the generation of Ezra. Nevertheless, the Masoretic notes do represent one of the oldest traditions for interpreting the text, which functions as a form of commentary.[15] In this study, the Masoretic division of the text will not be secondary but will be integral in terms of dividing and, therefore, interpreting the text. As I seek to understand the history of interpretation and why certain ideas about the text and its characters developed, I consider the present division and scholarly discussion of where ideas begin and end to be important.

Following the Masoretic markings is also relevant for discussing the beginnings and endings of the stories. As becomes clear in this study, the beginning and ending of the different stories relating to Sarah vary almost as much as the approaches taken to these texts. Yet what material scholars consider as part of any particular story affects the picture of Sarah and is key in understanding her role and function in the text. Therefore, I will pay a fair amount of attention to where any "chapter" begins and ends and how it relates to the surrounding stories.

Discussions of Sarah usually begin with the assumption that Abraham is the chosen one of the Israelite Deity.[16] Interpretors of the text hail him as the man of faith and ultimate hero in the story.[17] Thus, they use various devices to explain away Abraham's actions that are problematic for a modern audience.[18] Recently, scholars have questioned this approach to Abraham.[19] The present study does not assume that the traditional interpretation is wrong; it only asks the reader to retain an open mind on the status of Abraham, the legitimacy of his actions, his relationship with Sarah and Lot, and how he deals with his Deity.

One might argue that it is impossible to see the entire life of Sarah or evaluate her completely because the text was not written to discuss the story of Sarah: she serves as a character in someone else's story. This is a valid argument and, as a result, my study investigates texts where Sarah's name appears and/or she has some actions along with passages where she does not appear. I consider the connecting units in evaluating Sarah, something that has generally not been done, because these connecting passages reveal much about the characters with whom Sarah associates and impact how they view her. Since many of these characters are developing along with the story, we need to consider their new statuses and attitudes. In the development of the story, Sarah deals with the individual characters as they change, and we must take this into account when evaluating her. In fact, I argue that the connecting stories function intentionally as comparative material and are integral to the reader's evaluation of the other characters in the story.

This study focuses primarily on the character of Sarah, but it is impossible to investigate her without also considering the roles of Abraham, Lot, the Israelite Deity, Hagar, Ishmael, and Isaac. Sarah's life and the story recounted about her in the text are part of the book of Genesis, where these players have prominent roles. Furthermore, because of her status as a woman and wife in a patriarchal system, any discussion without considering these characters would not be evaluating what options were available to her.

Other themes emerging in the study of Sarah include the role of foreshadowing in the text. Scholars have periodically observed foreshadowing in a few places but have seldom considered the extent of foreshadowing in the various stories surrounding Sarah. The primary themes of foreshadowing I identify in this study are the anticipation of the exodus from Egypt and the future role of King David.

The author recognizes that the volume of literature on the topic of Sarah and Gen 11–24 is enormous. I do not pretend to refer to all of the available literature. Instead, I have chosen three major commentaries that represent, to a certain extent, a more standard traditional approach to the biblical text. Thus, I respond and react chiefly to the commentaries by Brueggemann, Speiser, and von Rad.[20] My reasons for choosing these three, despite the fact that they are a bit older than some recent possibilities, are based on a number of considerations. These three volumes represent slightly different methodological approaches to a commentary: theological (Brueggemann), ancient Near Eastern/philological (Speiser), and a 1949 definition of literary criticism (von Rad). The three authors continue to be influential in the field, and their commentaries still serve as the basis of much of biblical scholarship. Despite these significant differences, their scholarship has a number of similarities. These volumes predate feminist concerns and are not cognizant of them; to a large extent they precede a newer wave of scholarship that considers the text as a unified document with a continuous narrative—the approach taken here. We could consider these three commentaries to be outdated on some levels.

Yet they still hold prominence in the field and exercise a great influence on later scholarship. Hence, they are appropriate representatives of what could be considered a traditional approach to the text.

I want also to bring in as much ancient Near Eastern and archaeological data as possible. Nevertheless, much of this data is difficult to access from many libraries. As a result, the author has relied on the *Anchor Bible Dictionary* (*ABD*) for a great deal of material, rather than citing many other volumes.[21] There are a number of reasons for this choice. The *ABD* is a fairly recent publication. Though there are many dictionaries of the Bible, most of them are one-volume publications, providing shorter articles and less bibliography than *ABD*. To a large extent, because of the definition of the volume as a "dictionary," most entries represent the middle of the road in scholarly opinion, though this is not the case for all articles in *ABD*. The essays in *ABD* usually close with a basic bibliography; if the reader wants to do more research, the references offered in *ABD* should lead them to other sources.

The results of this study reveal much about Sarah and modern scholarship. What I make clear in this study is that Sarah is as much chosen by the Deity as is Abraham. This becomes apparent when viewing the role of Sarah in the promise, Abraham's actions with Sarah and with others around him, the Deity's role in the interactions between Sarah and Abraham, the legacy Sarah leaves, and Abraham's actions following Sarah's death.

Notes

1. Sarah's name in Gen 11–17 is Sarai, which is not changed till chapter 17. Despite this, when making general statements, we will call her Sarah, but in chapters before Gen 17 refer to her as Sarai.

2. P. Trible, "Hagar: The Desolation of Rejection," in *Texts of Terror: Literary-Feminist Readings of Biblical Narratives* (Overtures to Biblical Theology 13; Philadelphia: Fortress, 1984), 9–36, is one of the first and most influential studies to portray her in this manner. Yet D. W. Cotter, *Genesis* (Berit Olam; Collegeville: Liturgical Press, 2003), 104, has recently defined her as "cruel."

3. E. Fuchs, "The Literary Characterization of Mothers and Sexual Politics in the Hebrew Bible," in *Feminist Perspectives on Biblical Scholarship* (ed. A. Yarbro Collins; Atlanta: Scholars Press, 1985), 117–36.

4. P. Trible, "Genesis 22: The Sacrifice of Sarah," in *Women in the Hebrew Bible: A Reader* (ed. A. Bach; New York: Routledge, 1999), 271–92.

5. Ibid. On my use of "Deity," see n. 16, below.

6. K. Pfisterer Darr, "More than the Stars of the Heavens: Critical, Rabbinical, and Feminist Perspectives on Sarah," in *Far More Precious Than Jewels: Perspectives on Biblical Women* (Gender and the Biblical Tradition; Louisville: Westminster/ John Knox Press, 1991), 85–131.

7. S. Teubal, *Sarah the Priestess: The First Matriarch of Genesis* (Athens, Ohio: Ohio University Press, 1984).

8. R. Christopher Heard, *Dynamics of Diselection: Ambiguity in Genesis 12–36 and Ethnic Boundaries in Post-Exilic Judah* (Atlanta: Society of Biblical Literature, 2001), 25–96.

9. S. Pace Jeansonne, *The Women of Genesis: From Sarah to Potiphar's Wife* (Minneapolis: Augsburg Fortress, 1990), 1.

10. For a brief introduction to biblical criticism, see Roy A. Harrisville, "Biblical Criticism," *Eerdmans Dictionary of the Bible* (ed. D. N. Freedman; Grand Rapids: Eerdmans, 2000), 183–86.

11. E.J. Revell, "Masorah," *ABD* 4:592.

12. E.J. Revell, "Masoretes," *ABD* 4:593.

13. E.J. Revell, "Masoretic Text," *ABD* 4:599.

14. E.J. Revell, "Masorah," *ABD* 4:592.

15. E.J. Revell, "Masoretes," *ABD* 4:594.

16. The Hebrew Bible presents the role that the Israelite Deity chooses for Abraham in a number of different ways in the text. Interpreters often lift up Gen 15:6, where "Abraham believed in the Deity, and he credited it to him as righteousness." This is usually considered the clearest case because it is coupled with Rom 4:1–3, a New Testament example, in such common references as the *Anchor Bible Dictionary [ABD]* (ed. D. N. Freedman; 6 vols.; New York: Doubleday, 1992). See A. R. Millard, "Abraham," *ABD* 1:35–41.

Notice that throughout the text I will refer to the entity written in the Hebrew as YHWH as "the Deity" or "the Israelite Deity." This is not done to insult the divine but rather to protect people's personal relationship with the divine. YHWH is the only character in Genesis with whom most modern readers have some sort of a personal relationship. As a result, God is the one character in the book whom people "know." It is much more difficult to gain a clear understanding of how this character functions in the book, especially in relationships with the other characters, when using this particular character's modern name (God). Using the term "the Deity" distances that specific character from our personal relationships and places the character on a footing more similar to the others in the book.

17. "The Tradition affirms Abraham as a 'knight of faith' who does trust." W. Brueggemann, *Genesis* (Interpretation; Atlanta: John Knox, 1982), 111.

18. In a number of places in this study, I will elaborate on these devices.

19. A few particularly noteworthy cases are D. W. Cotter, *Genesis* (Berit Olam; Collegeville: Liturgical Press, 2003); T. Desmond Alexander, *Abraham in the Negev: A Source-critical Investigation of Genesis 20:1–22:19* (Carlisle, U.K.: Paternoster, 1997); and D. Nolan Fewell and D. Gunn, *Gender Power and Promise: The Subject of the Bible's First Story* (Nashville: Abingdon 1993).

20. W. Brueggemann, *Genesis*; E. A. Speiser, *Genesis: A New Translation with Introduction and Commentary* (Anchor Bible 1; Garden City, N.Y.: Doubleday, 1985); G. von Rad, *Genesis: A Commentary* (Old Testament Library; Philadelphia: Westminster, 1972). All three are in a series, in print, and easily available.

21. See n. 16, above.

CHAPTER 1

The Beginning of the Story: Genesis 11

One of the most important elements in understanding a story is where it begins. The beginning of Sarah's story is debated. The story of Sarah clearly is embedded in the book of Genesis, and readers have much discussion concerning how the text should be divided and the role of the genealogies within the text.[1] Where Sarah's story begins and how it relates to what came before her—these matters are important for understanding the role that she and her family play in the book of Genesis, especially as it relates to the so-called primeval history.

Scholarship sees a sharp break between the earlier chapters and the focus later in Genesis on Abraham and his family: "There is no doubt that in the construction of Genesis, a major break in the narrative is intended between 11:32 and 12:1. Indeed, it is perhaps the most important structural break in the Old Testament and certainly in Genesis."[2] A clear example is Claus Westermann's commentary on Genesis, where chapters 1–11 appear as volume 1 and chapters 12–36 as volume 2.[3] Though there are modern publishing reasons why one volume could not conveniently contain his massive study on Genesis, most other commentaries make a similar division.[4]

A shift in focus certainly appears between 1–11 and what follows. Yet there is little agreement as to precisely where that break occurs. Cotter and Speiser include the initial genealogical information about Abraham with the primeval history.[5] Von Rad includes Abraham's "origin and call" and "departure" as part of the biblical primeval history. Brueggemann includes verses 11:30–32 as part of Abraham's call because, "God does not begin the history of Israel ex nihilo. The history of promise does not emerge in a vacuum."[6] At issue is the transition, how tightly connected the two sections are, and what elements of chapter 11 are part of the transition.

Part of the dilemma is related to how one considers the role of genealogies. In the heyday of the documentary hypothesis, especially following Noth, scholars saw the genealogies as late secondary impositions on the text.[7] As a result, they did not stress the role of the genealogies in Genesis 11 for integrating the line of Terah–Abram to what previously happened in the text. In recent years scholars have questioned those notions.[8] Steinberg goes so far as to state, "It seems clear that the genealogies are primary in Genesis."[9] She sees the flow of the narrative units taking their meaning as a resolution to the problem of generation continuity, and thus identified within the genealogies.[10]

If such is the case, then the story of Sarah clearly begins in Gen 11. Even in this context, where the story begins within the chapter, the matter is not straightforward. Steinberg again goes against the traditional approach: "Through the structural analysis of parallel genealogies in Genesis it becomes possible to discern a shift in perspective from the general humankind to history of Israel not at the generation of Terah but of Shem in 11:10."[11] Further proof of the beginning of this new story, with its focus on one family beginning with 11:10, comes from Robinson's argument that the beginning of the Shem genealogy is an abrupt change from the catastrophic Babel incident (11:1–9).[12] The Masoretes see the breakdown in a similar way, with a major break following the Babel incident. They view the focus on the line of Terah as a new topic, even though the break is not larger than breaks between the other generations of Shem.

This study considers the beginning of Sarah's story to be in 11:10, following the Babel incident. The Babel incident is significant as the last story before Sarah appears, and Babel functions as a contrast to what happens with the family that becomes the focus of the rest of the book.

The story is situated in Babel. The similarity of the name Babel to the city of Babylon and the tower built to a ziggurat immediately place the story in Mesopotamia, for both modern and ancient readers. In this story, by building a tower to heaven humanity again confounds the Deity's plans to have them behave the way the Deity would like.[13] The reason for the building is to "make a name for ourselves; else we shall be scattered all over the world" (11:4). The Deity is not happy with humanity's actions because "nothing that they may propose to do will be out of their reach" (11:6). The Deity has recently promised not to destroy the earth again, at least not using the waters (9:11), and therefore is forced to spread humanity across the nations of the world and make them have different languages so that they will not understand each other.[14] This sets up the following stories, in which various nations populate the world visited by the patriarchs.

The story of Babel ends with people scattered, and the narrative continues in Babel, or the same region, though the text does not state this explicitly. Instead, it begins by recounting the line of Shem. The shift is rather abrupt. The text has already delineated the general line of Shem (10:21–31), much as it did for Shem's siblings Japheth (10:2–12) and Ham (10:12–20). One would expect the account again to recount the descendants of Noah in chapter 10, beginning with the eldest, but the opposite occurs. The list begins with the youngest, Japheth, then moves to Ham, and finishes with Shem, the oldest. Could even this be foreshadowing that the concept of primogeniture is not in place in Genesis, or rather, that the idea continues not to function in Genesis since the Deity has rejected the sacrifice of Cain, the older brother, while accepting the younger, Abel's, sacrifice (4:1–5)? Another option is that Noah's children's descendants are listed from youngest to oldest so that the list would end with Shem, the beginning point of the next unit and focus of the narrative in general. Of course, both ideas could be operating intentionally and simultaneously.

The reference to the line of Shem, the tower of Babel story, and Abram is a nice bit of foreshadowing for Abram's story and another wordplay.[15] The wordplay is rooted in the meaning "name" for *shem* in Hebrew. The people in Gen 11 build the tower in the first place to "make a name for ourselves; else we shall be scattered" (11:4). The irony is that the very act of building the tower to make the name is what leads the Deity to scatter the people in the first place (11:5–9). In the following genealogy Abram is part of the line of Shem (name), the son of Noah. Finally, in Gen 12:2 one of the reasons the Deity provides Abram that he should leave is that the Deity promises to make Abram's name (*shem*) great. Here the emphasis seems to be on the idea that the Deity is the one who will make someone's name great, not the people's own actions, especially a building project. This idea becomes lost when readers separate the genealogy of Gen 11 from the account of Gen 12.

The genealogy of the line of Shem is standard and somewhat monotonous. The list begins with the name of a figure and the number of years they lived before the birth of their heir. Then the text lists the heir's birth, the age of the main character, and the number of the character's children. The next unit begins with the heir mentioned in the previous unit. This genealogy is similar to the one already seen in Gen 5:6–27, though the list in Gen 5 provides a final summary of years lived and notification of the person's death.

As with the list in Gen 5, the final name in the list of Gen 11 has the same introduction as the previous cases: the text introduces the name in the discussion of the father. The additional information in the body of the character's reference indicates that this person is different. Also, as with Noah, the person with whom the list stops has three sons listed by name. As in the Noah announcement, the text gives only one year for the sons' birth, though it does not present them as triplets, and the order in which they are listed appears to be their birth order.[16]

Thus, the genealogical beginning in Gen 11:10 establishes a break with the previous story and what has happened before the focus on the line of Shem; yet it still does not depart radically from what is in the text thus far. The Deity creates humans, who repeatedly do not do what the Deity would like. The Deity repeatedly sends punishments to correct the situation.[17] The Deity even tries to rid the earth of all the problems and focus on one family, and still that does not work. Once again, as with the Noah situation, the Deity will focus on one family, but this time the Deity has a new plan.

Where to Begin, Genesis 11:26 or 11:27?

Most scholars see the role of this unit as introductory but debate the nature of its introductory character. Furthermore, whereas the earlier sentences tied the text to the previous elements of Genesis, this unit also functions as a bridge by its relationship to the other genealogical list.

The first question is whether this unit begins in 11:26 or 11:27. A few different translations reflect the problem. According to the Masoretes and NJPS, Gen 11:26 begins a new paragraph with the discussion of the new family. According to *BHS* and King James Version (KJV), the new paragraph begins with line 27. The Revised Standard Version (RSV) avoids the problem to some extent by having 11:26 stand alone as its own paragraph, thus beginning a new unit with 11:27. Speiser treats 11:26 and

11:27 as their own paragraphs and sees a large break between 11:27 and 11:28.[18] The differences concern the relationship of this unit/s with the previous verses and the focus of the following unit. By beginning a new unit with 11:26, the focus of at least this unit is on Terah. It concerns Terah and the children he bears, and the rest of the unit is an elaboration of that concept. Genesis 11:27 introduces the concept of descendants and generations through the use of the term *toledot* (generations). The trouble with the following generation is even suggested through the introduction of Lot into the narrative. Thus, if Terah is the primary focus of the unit, then it must begin in Gen 11:26; if the future of the line is the focus, then Gen 11:27 is the true starting point.

The opening verse of the story relates to a point touched on earlier: the role of the genealogies in Genesis and the biblical text in general. According to Steinberg, "The initial genealogy of each family cycle can function as a superscription or a prologue in the stereotypical language beginning with the phrase 'this is the history of the family of.'"[19] According to this understanding, the story would begin with Gen 11:27. Steinberg further states: "The plot of Genesis 11:10–50:26 unfolds through narratives that are set within a genealogical framework. The narratives and genealogical framework together organize the plot of generational continuity."[20] Such an analysis sees "Gen 11:10–32 as the introduction to the stories in 12:1–25:11, Gen 25:12–26 as introduction to 25:27–35:29 and 36:1–43 as introduction to remaining narratives in Genesis."[21]

If the beginning is so clearly 11:27, why did scholars such as the Masoretes begin with 11:26? Beginning with Gen 11:26 raises the importance of Terah. The following few lines are more about him and what happens to his descendants, rather than making the following generation the key participants. This understanding has a great deal in its favor and does not necessarily minimize the importance of the later generation. By beginning with Terah, he is likened to Noah, who also had three sons. The text says a fair amount about Noah and recognizes that he has some merits (6:8–9); but the text says litle about Terah. Yet Terah may be more important than traditionally considered. He begins the journey to Canaan, though the text is silent as to why. Abram is important to the development of the nation of Israel, but it is Terah's descendants who are crucial for the continuation of the family line. The importance of Terah's line is clear in the search for an heir (considering Lot, discussed in more detail later) and as a source for future progeny for Abram's descendants (Nahor, ancestor of Rebekah; 22:20–23). Thus, all of Terah's children are important, relevant, and included in the future of Israel, a point high-lighted by beginning the unit in Gen 11:26.

The difficulty in determining the true beginning of the unit again shows how closely tied this unit is to what precedes it. The focus on Terah and/or Abram begins by tying him/them to the genealogy of Shem, which flows directly from the flood and Babel incidents. Previously in the book the genealogical unit introduces the line of Seth, and this is just another permutation of that same type of unit. While the text introduces something new, it does so in a way that ties it directly to what precedes it.

Genesis 11:26–32

Even if one considers Gen 11:27 to be the beginning, the focus concerns the family of Terah and its continuity. Genesis 11:26 introduces Terah's children: Abram, Nahor, and Haran. The following verse, Gen 11:27, introduces the concept of the next generation through Lot, son of Haran. On one level this appears somewhat analogous to Noah and his children's descendants in that it introduces, presumably, the offspring of the young-est child first, though the following verses contradict this understanding. Still, the introduction of Lot is unusual. He is introduced in 11:27, not with the generation into which he is born, for reasons that are not appar-ent until 11:28, which reports his father's death. What his introduction in 11:27 establishes is his importance to the unfolding plot. Lot appears in the text even before the wives in the generation of Terah's children or the children of any of that first generation. From a narrative perspective, "The flow of the narrative units takes its meaning as a resolution to the prob-lem of generational continuity identified within the genealogies. Gene-alogy to family reproduction to genealogies is the way for literature to express the passage from generation to generation."[22] Ironically, here the text introduces the next generation for no apparent reason, creating al-most an overabundance of heirs for the next generation.

The following verse (11:28) first establishes the reason for Lot's importance, or at least the first hint at Lot's role: his father dies "before" Terah. The term 'al p'nêy is open to a number interpretations. The range of interpretations is on some levels rather narrow and obvious, yet the variations may be more significant. For example, according to NJPS and Speiser, Haran died "in the lifetime of" his father. According to KJV and RSV, Haran died "before" his father, meaning either "before his eyes" or "before he died." The LXX understands it as Haran dying "in the pres-ence of Terah," meaning Terah was there when it happened. In most interpretations the issue is not one of significance since the general thrust of the statement is that Haran died before Terah did, which explains Lot's attachment to Abram, leading them to travel together and leading Abram to consider him an heir. We might consider the rest of the sentence simply as an explanation or reminder of where the family is when these events occur and/or as an introduction to where the family lives, Ur of the Chaldees.

The reference (11:28) may have more to it since, according to the notes about how long Terah lives and when various events in Abram's life occur, Terah is alive for quite a long time, including such important events in Abram's life as the birth of both Ishmael and Isaac.[23] The focus of the verse may be on the death of Haran in Ur of the Chaldeans. The other possibility could be a focus on the children's association with their father. The biblical text mentions Terah's death before it portrays Abram leaving Haran (11:32; 12:1); but according to the rest of the information about when events happen, Terah is not dead when Abram leaves Haran (in northwest Mesopotamia).[24] This would mean that Abram left the presence of his father and never returned. Even von Rad does not find satisfying the conjecture that combining several strands of texts created this "inconsistency in the text."[25] He does not resolve the dilemma, but he does question the unnaturalness of Abram's departure "from his father's house" (12:1).[26] Again, the text does not highlight the fact that Terah is alive when most of the events that happen to Abram are narrated in the text, yet the reference to Haran's death "before" Terah may hint at the idea.

The reference (11:28) also contains the same terminology used in the famous line in 12:1, where the Deity commands Abram to leave. There the Deity tells Abram to leave his 'erets (land), his moledet (place of birth), and the house of his father. Genesis 11:28 informs the reader that Haran, Abram's brother, dies in the 'erets of his moledet in Ur of the Chaldees before his father—thus "before his father" in 11:28 parallels "your father's house" in 12:1. As a result, both Abram and Haran leave, but they take different routes. It also shifts the role and importance of Nahor, who is the ancestor of the women that Abram's descendents marry, since he is the one who remains with Terah. Ironically, Nahor does not leave Ur with the rest of the family (11:31), or the text does not mention it, but he later appears to have settled in Aram-Naharaim (at the city of Nahor, near Haran; 24:10). That is where Abraham's servant later finds a wife for Isaac from among the descendants of Nahor (24:24).

The other component introduced in this verse is Ur of the Chaldees. The text reads that Haran died in the land of his birth, in Ur of the

Chaldees. The reference to Ur of the Chaldees is important yet slightly odd for this time of the book and is clearly an element of foreshadowing. Ur is a city in southern Mesopotamia that was particularly important in the third millennium B.C.E.[27] The reference to "of the Chaldees" is clearly a first millennium reference since the Chaldeans appear on the scene in the end of the second millennium and only become significant in the first millennium.[28] The thrust of the reference could be to clarify which Ur is referenced here, but because of the role and status of Ur, Chaldeans, and the later Babylonians, the reference carries much more weight than that of merely placing the city for the reader.

"Chaldeans is a term that strictly belongs to first millennium and its use here may deliberately make the point that Israel has returned to the land that Abram was called from."[29] If such is the case, the impact of an exilic audience knowing that they have returned to the starting point is a powerful statement. One can read it in a number of ways, all of them important. Is it saying that the exilic audience, like Abram, should return to Israel? Or does it also say that Judah started there, now they are back, and maybe that is where they should be? Both possibilities are far removed from each other, and everything in between is possible; hence, it is difficult to date such a text or understand its impact on its ancient audience. For the larger story of Genesis–Kings (if such is a story that should be considered in any way continuous), the reference places the Israelites exactly where they started. For the story of Abram, it introduces the term "Ur of the Chaldees" and leaves open the question of whether Abram actually did all that is commissioned in 12:1, where neither the name Ur nor the name Chaldees appears.

Only after the text establishes the origination of the family and Haran's death does it introduce Sarai (11:29). The same verse also names Milcah as the wife of Nahor. Both women are crucial for the continuation of the line, and both appear equally at this point in the story. Interestingly enough, while Lot apparently is already alive and his father dead, there is no mention of his mother's name. In a text where the role of mothers is so crucial, and if we are to understand Lot as a potential heir, one might expect her name at least, but the text does not discuss her at all. Lot thus becomes the only one from his generation, the same as for Isaac and Ishmael, with no named mother. Are we to understand that Lot never really is an intended heir to the Deity's promise?[30]

At this point, the text reveals more about Milcah than Sarai by mentioning Milcah's parentage. Milcah is defined as the daughter of Haran, the father of Milcah and Iscah (11:29). This verse has raised a number of

questions concerning the reason for mentioning Milcah's father and what
her relationship is to the deceased Haran. Already von Rad thinks it
strange that Milcah's father is named but not the father of the much more
important Sarai.[31] One answer to the problem may be in the Abimelech
story, where Abraham claims that Sarah is truly his sister in that they
both have the same father, though different mothers (20:12). Nevertheless, the veracity of Abraham's claim at that point is questionable and will
be examined later in this study. Another possibility for referring to Milcah's parentage is to fool the reader into thinking that Sarai is not the
important one at all. In fact, it is only in Gen 17 that the Deity singles
Sarah out as the one who will bear the relevant heir to the Deity's promise. Up until that point there are many questions about whether Sarai will
be the mother of an heir (and there are still many questions following
Gen 17). The reference to Milcah's parentage further contributes to asking whether Sarai is the person who will carry out the Deity's plans for
Abram's descendants.

The question still remains concerning what the text says about Milcah's father. She is *bat haran*, the "daughter of Haran," though this could
also mean "a woman from the city of Haran," since later the entire family moves to the city Haran (11:31). The text further names Haran as the
father of Milcah and Iscah. Since the reader just learned that Haran, the
brother of Abram, dies while still in Ur and that he has a son (Lot), is this
his daughter? According to Speiser, Nahor marries the daughter of his
deceased brother Haran, his niece.[32] Cassuto offered the opposite interpretation, that the reason Iscah is mentioned is so the reader knows that
Nahor's father-in-law Haran is not the same individual as his brother
Haran.[33] All of this is complicated by the lack of information on Iscah.
Since she disappears after this verse, her mention here further complicates the reference.

According to Speiser, "These laconic notices by J presuppose a very
ancient tradition precisely because they seem to be pointless in the present context."[34] But are they pointless? Nahor's marriage to his niece may
indicate some sort of protection for her. It may also serve as a foreshadowing of Abram's relationship with Lot: Nahor marries the daughter of
his deceased brother, Haran, and Abram takes Haran's son, Lot. If so, this
may be a sign that the reader should understand Lot as a potential heir
for Abram.

Aside from Abram, the reference to Milcah's parentage highlights her
role in the story from the beginning. Though the text does not mention
her often, her introduction comes with notice of her ancestry. This keeps

the reader from being confused when later in the story (22:20–22) the narrator relates that Milcah too has borne children. Her children's children are important for the continuation of the line and the story of Rebekah, Milcah's granddaughter, who becomes the wife of Isaac (24:67). Abraham emphasizes that Isaac must not marry a Canaanite (24:3) and thus places stress on the importance of Isaac's wife, who will become the mother for the future descendants of the patriarchal line.

The reference to Milcah, and her apparent importance because of the reference to her family line (whatever it may mean), is in stark contrast to Sarai. The sentence introducing the wives lists no paternity for Sarai (11:29), and while the following verse is devoted entirely to her, it introduces a major problem: she is barren and has no child (11:30). Though von Rad points out that the reference to Sarai's barrenness is mentioned "only in passing," this verse clearly is essential for understanding what happens to Sarai and how to understand her in the following stories.[35] It is the first reference to her alone and establishes her role in the story: a barren woman married to a man whose promise is to his offspring. Thus, most of the following narrative concerning Sarai focuses on her barren state. As usual, we must first understand the thrust of a biblical verse before we can understand its role in the narrative.

On some levels the translation is rather simple, but even here there are some questions. The verse 11:30 begins with a *vav* consecutive, which could be translated as either "but,"[36] "and," or even "now."[37] Though the difference is somewhat minimal, the issue affects how we relate this verse to what precedes it. Beginning with "and" or "now" implies that the information conveyed is somewhat new in topic, as though there had been a slight shift in focus. Beginning the verse with "but" indicates that the verse is related directly to what went before it and is somehow in contrast to it. If there is clearly a contrast between the two verses (11:29–30), the "but" indicates that the contrast concerns issues raised in the previous verse. For this to be the case here, the discussion of Sarai in Gen 11:30 should concern her parentage, as 11:29 does for Milcah. While the verse continues to discuss family matters, its concern is with future children, not past family connections.

Second, the verse (11:30) is repetitive. If Sarai is barren, why does the text also state that she has no offspring? In fact, the second half of the verse is a hapax legomenon in the MT, the only place where *valad* is used, meaning "offspring, child."[38] The text is stressing a point. Milcah has family; Sarai has none to speak of, and from 11:30 it seems highly unlikely that she will have any. This contrast not only establishes how different the two are but also sets up Sarai's character from the beginning. According to Trible, "Unique and barren Sarai . . . has neither pedigree or fertility, neither past nor future."[39] She further states that Sarai "threatens the demise of genealogy."[40] She is an outsider with no apparent use to Abram, something that shall be reinforced by Abram/Abraham throughout the text. He leaves it to the Deity to protect Sarai and later in the story to establish her as the matriarch.

Genesis 11:30 establishes Sarai's role in the ensuing saga and also introduces a major issue that the story needs to resolve: who will be Abram's heir? According to Steinberg, "Heirship questions introduced in genealogies of men depend for their resolution upon matters relating to women (their status, fertility, and, to some extent, choice)."[41] In the larger story, "Shem, Ishmael, Esau show the natural flow of a family line, not so in Terah, Isaac, and Jacob where there is a crisis in heirship and therefore text/narrative focused on working out the problem."[42] She goes on to state, "The plot of Genesis 11:10–50:26 unfolds through narratives that are set within a genealogical framework. The narratives and genealogical framework together organize the plot of generational continuity."[43] By introducing Sarai's childbearing problems, the story sets the plot for the next few chapters. If generational continuity is part of the major plot for this part of Genesis, then we must consider Sarai a major character since her fertility issues are one of the significant elements in establishing the dilemma.

It is possible to argue that, at this point, the focus of the text is still not on Abram and who will be his descendant, but on which line of Terah will continue. At this point in the story, the reader is still engrossed in the genealogy of Terah, not Abram. One of Terah's children already is deceased, though he has at least one son and possibly two daughters. It is also possible that Nahor is married to the daughter of the deceased brother. Abram, on the other hand, is married to someone with no past and apparently, because of her barren state, no future. Steinberg claims that this is part of "the problem of heirship that makes questionable the future of Terah's descendants through the line of Abram."[44] She further claims that Sarai's barrenness, with the awkward manner in which Lot's name suddenly occurs in 11:27, suggests that the future of the second generation will probably be secured through Lot.[45]

The focus on Terah as the clan leader who will carry on his line continues through the next two verses. In 11:31 Terah leaves Ur. The text clarifies who leaves as his son Abram; his grandson Lot, the son of Haran; and his daughter-in-law Sarai—in case readers forgot, she again is named as Abram's wife. The text does not list Nahor and his family with those who leave Ur. Ironically, when Abram later sends to find a wife for Isaac, he directs his servant to Aram-Naharaim, where Nahor is then living (24:10). Thus, at some point that part of the family also leaves Ur. Is it to join the elderly Terah at Haran? While it is not integral to the story and not mentioned in most discussions, it could be relevant concerning Abram's relationship to Terah in the following story.

The verse reports that Terah sets out from Ur of the Chaldees for Canaan but that they settle in Haran (11:31). The text provides no reason for Terah's departure or why they stopped in Haran. According to the book of Joshua, Terah worshipped other gods, and then the Deity sent Abraham to Canaan (Josh 24:2–3). The Joshua reference places this story with the family of Terah by saying that Terah was the father of both Abraham and Nahor, but it does little to explain why Terah left Ur or why he stopped in Haran. What is clear is that the family was on their way to Canaan *before* Abram received his call. It also calls into question what exactly the Deity later asks Abram to do (Gen 12:1) and whether he completely followed the Deity's instructions.

The final verse of Gen 11, concerning the death of Terah, occurs just before a major break, after which Abram receives the call from the Deity. The verse says that the days of Terah were 205 years and that he died in Haran. The following chapter, where Abram leaves, follows a natural progression: his father dies, and the story then focuses on Abram, the heir to Terah. But according to the information in the story, such is not the case. Though the placement of Terah's death fits neatly into the story line, the numbers do not add up. Why does the text want Terah dead at this point? According to the information the text provides, Terah is not dead when Abram leaves Haran/Ur, when he goes to Egypt, when he battles the foreign kings, when Ishmael is born, or even when Isaac is born. In fact, if Isaac is forty years old when he weds Rebekah (25:20), then Terah has died a mere four years earlier. It is clear that the text is trying to minimize this fact of overlapping life spans. Placing the reference to Terah's death before Abram's departure makes a clean break. It hides the fact that Abram abandons his father, while apparently Nahor stays with him. At the same time, if we understand Terah as dead when Abram receives his call from the Deity, then it also lessens the difficulty of what he is called to do—leave his father's house.

Terah's departure may tie the story back again to the tower of Babel. Did Terah leave as part of the scattering described following that incident (11:8)? If so, then the backtracking to Shem's line, already mentioned in

Gen 10, is a means of describing the type of people scattered in that passage (11:8). The text does not stress why Terah leaves or who specifically is scattered. Clearly, the specifics are not the concern of the text. At the same time the text drops enough hints to keep the reader wondering.

Conclusions

Scholars can divide the book of Genesis in a number of different ways and have done so throughout their history. Despite the break between chapters 11 and 12, clear connections exist through the story of the tower of Babel, the genealogy of Shem, and the introduction of Terah and his family. The turn to Abram in Gen 12 is not a sudden burst of interest in one individual but is part of a progression to narrowing the focus to one line.

The later emphasis on Abram should probably be seen as connected quite closely to the events in Gen 11. In the tower of Babel story, the Deity reacts to the notion that humans might determine their own greatness. As the next chapter of this study makes clear, the Deity emphasizes making Abram great. Thus far, nothing about Abram in particular highlights him as anything special, and yet he becomes the recipient of the Deity's promise. Is this because of something innately wonderful about Abram, or about the Deity? As this study continues it becomes more apparent that the point of Abram is that the Deity can make even Abram great.

The case with Sarai is slightly different. The text has already introduced information about her that seems to indicate that she of all people is not the correct one to be the mother of the heir to the promise: she is barren. Her actions—at least from a perspective that will develop in this study—do not appear as controversial as some of Abram's actions while following the Deity's instructions and trying to turn them into reality. Thus, her situation does not completely parallel that of Abram's. The two are similar in that, with the information the text has introduced thus far, there is nothing about either Abram or Sarai that would lead one to envision either one as prime choices for the Deity's plan. Their humble beginnings may specifically be in order to emphasize the Deity's plans for them.

Notes

1. For a brief introduction to genealogies in the biblical text, see Robert R. Wilson, "Genealogy, Genealogies," *ABD* 2:932.

2. W. Brueggemann, *Genesis* (Interpretation; Atlanta: John Knox, 1982), 116.

3. C. Westermann, *Genesis*, vol. 2: *Genesis 12–36* (Neukirchen-Vluyn: Neukirchener Verlag, 1981).

4. General examples include Brueggemann, *Genesis*, part 1: "The 'Pre-History': The Sovereign Call of God"; E. A. Speiser, *Genesis* (Anchor Bible 1; Garden City, N.Y.: Doubleday, 1985), names Gen 1–11 "Primeval History"; and G. von Rad, *Genesis: A Commentary* (Old Testament Library; Philadelphia: Westminster, 1972), calls it "The Biblical Primeval History." Even the recent volume by D. W. Cotter, *Genesis* (Berit Olam; Collegeville: Liturgical Press, 2003), names it "Studies about Beginnings: Gen 1–11."

5. Speiser, *Genesis*; Cotter, *Genesis*.

6. Brueggemann, *Genesis*, 116.

7. M. Noth, *A History of Pentateuchal Traditions* (Englewood Cliffs, N.J.: Prentice-Hall, 1972), 214–19.

8. N. Steinberg, *Kinship and Marriage in Genesis: A Household Economics Perspective* (Minneapolis: Fortress, 1993), 39–45.

9. Ibid., 2.

10. Ibid., 40.

11. Ibid., 41.

12. R. B. Robinson, "Literary Functions of the Genealogies of Genesis," *CBQ* 48 (1986): 601–2.

13. Thus far in Genesis other incidents also portray humans not appearing to follow what the Deity intends: Adam and Eve, Cain and Abel, Lamech, and before the flood just about everyone other than Noah. It is not clear whether they are responsible for not knowing what the Deity wants of them, since the text does not have the Deity telling the various characters how to behave, with the exception of Adam, who had only one rule to follow (Gen 2:17).

14. Nowhere in the Pentateuch is language a barrier to communication. There are references to using dialect for trying to identify a person's tribe in order to kill them, such as the shibboleth/sibboleth incident in Judg 12:1–6; and the Rabshakeh episode in 2 Kgs 18:19–37 reveals that some people do not understand all languages. Despite these episodes, the text never identifies language as a barrier to communication.

15. This study will call Abram and Sarai by those names when that is how the text refers to them; following their name changes I will use their new names, Abraham and Sarah, so that this study is consistent with the biblical text.

16. While there is no explicit information concerning whether these are triplets or not, in the Noah story there are references to birth order, though they too are somewhat confused. Japheth is listed as the third son when referring to the three in order of Shem, Ham, and Japheth (Gen 5:32; 9:18; 10:1). Yet in Gen 9:24 the text claims that Ham is Noah's youngest son.

17. The punishments of the Deity thus far include the following: "cursing" the man or Adam and the serpent (Gen 3:14–17), expelling Adam from the garden of Eden (3:23–24), sending the flood (6:5–8:12), and changing languages and scattering the people after the tower of Babel incident (11:1–9).

18. Speiser, *Genesis*, 77.

19. Steinberg, *Kinship and Marriage*, 42.

20. Ibid., 36.

21. Ibid., 39.

22. Ibid., 40

23. Terah's age at death is based on the information in Genesis. According to Gen 11:26 Terah has lived 70 years when he fathers his sons. Then 11:32 says, "The days of Terah were 205 years." When Hagar bears Ishmael, 16:16 reports that Abraham is 86, thus meaning that Terah would be 156 years old and still living. At the birth of Isaac (Gen 21:5) Abraham is 100 years old, so Terah must be 176. The text does not say how old Abram/Abraham is at events other than his death.

24. Y. Zakovitch, "The Exodus from Ur of Chaldeans: A Chapter in Literary Archaeology," in *Ki Baruch Hu: Ancient Near Eastern Studies in Honor of Baruch A. Levine* (ed. R. Chazan, W. W. Hallo, L. H. Schiffman; Winona Lake: Eisenbrauns, 1999), 429. The Samaritan Pentateuch has Terah dying at age 145, meaning that Terah dies soon after reaching Haran, thus explaining why he cannot continue to Canaan. Acts 7:4 follows the same line of reasoning, which contradicts the information in the MT of Genesis.

25. Von Rad, *Genesis*, 158.

26. Ibid.

27. Since the site of Ur has been excavated, there is a fair amount of data about it from an archaeological perspective. For a beginning bibliography, see S. Pollack, "Ur," *The Oxford Encyclopedia of Archaeology in the Near East* (ed. E. M. Meyers; New York: Oxford University Press, 1997), 288–91; R. L. Zettler and L. Horne, *Treasures from the Royal Tombs of Ur* (Philadelphia: University Museum of Archaeology and Anthropology, 1998); and P. R. S. Moorey, *Ur "Of the Chaldees": A Revised and Updated Edition of Sir Leonard Woolley's Excavations at Ur* (Ithaca: Cornell University Press, 1982).

28. R. S. Hess, "Chaldea," *ABD* 1:886–87.

29. J. Goldingay, "The Patriarchs in Scripture and History," *Essays on Patriarchal Narratives* (ed. A. R. Millard and D. J. Wiseman; Leicester: Inter-Varsity Press, 1980), 25.

30. R. Christopher-Heard argues that the text introduces little about Lot here because the only reason to mention him at this point is to explain why he is with Abram later in the story. See R. Christopher-Heard, *Dynamics of Diselection: Ambiguity in Genesis 12–36 and Ethnic Boundaries in Post-Exilic Judah* (Atlanta: Society of Biblical Literature, 2001), 26.

31. Von Rad, *Genesis*, 158.

32. Speiser, *Genesis*, 78.

33. G. A. Rendsburg, *The Redaction of Genesis* (Winona Lake: Eisenbrauns, 1986), 30, quoting Umberto Cassuto (1883–1951).

34. Speiser, *Genesis*, 78.

35. Von Rad, *Genesis*, 158.

36. LXX, RSV, KJV.

37. NJPS.

38. BDB, 409. In some oriental manuscripts 2 Sam 6:23 contains a qere for this word that would result in the same consonantal form, though vocalized differently.

39. P. Trible, "Genesis 22: The Sacrifice of Sarah," in *Women in the Hebrew Bible: A Reader* (ed. A. Bach; New York: Routledge, 1999), 281.

40. Ibid., 281.

41. Steinberg, *Kinship and Marriage*, 45.

42. Ibid., 43.

43. Ibid., 38.

44. Ibid., 47.

45. Ibid., 47.

CHAPTER 2

Establishing Relationships: Genesis 12–13

According to most scholars, a new section of Genesis begins with chapter 12, despite its close ties to the preceding material.[1] The Masoretes also see Gen 12 as a new beginning by starting a new parashah (reading).[2] The chapter contains what is traditionally considered the Deity's call to Abram and the initial promise. It is less clear where the section ends, and therefore what information should be considered relevant to the call. Most scholars see a major break following 12:9, with the story of Abram in Egypt. Another break is assumed at the beginning of chapter 13, following the departure from Egypt, though there is less agreement among scholars about precisely where that break should appear.

All of this relates directly to understanding Sarai: one of the few major episodes concerning her occurs in the middle of this textual block (Gen 12). Traditionally, scholars treat these verses in three separate parts and therefore seldom examine how Sarai's stay in Egypt affects the story of the relationships among Abram, Lot, and Sarai. Yet in order to understand the development of the story, and in particular Sarai's character, one must consider the information as a unified section, as the Masoretes did.

This block of material covers Abram's call to travel to a new land, his arrival in Canaan, his sojourn into Egypt, and his separation from Lot. From this description it would appear that it has little to do with the focus of this book: Sarah. Yet Sarai is intimately connected to the call and the promise made to Abram; she is the one most at risk in Egypt, and she is the source of Abram's status there. Though she does not appear in Gen 13 (where Abram and Lot part ways), Abram's actions with Lot—compared to the previous episode in Egypt—establish a pattern that is followed in their relationship throughout the text.

Abram and the Call: Genesis 12:1–9

The first line of chapter 12 is well known: the Deity calls Abram to leave. While the Hebrew is not particularly difficult, there are some subtleties to the translation that are relevant for understanding what is being asked of Abram. In this verse the Deity tells Abram, literally, "You go yourself," though traditionally it is translated as "Go," or "Go forth."[3] The difference could be considered minor, but the Deity clearly is speaking to Abram and stresses him. Readers wonder whether he should take people with him, or whether the Deity commands him to go alone. The point may seem minor, but as the story progresses there are a number of situations where it is not clear that Abram actually is following the Deity's instructions. If the Deity initially commands Abram to go alone, then Abram already is modifying the Deity's plans by taking others along.

The rest of the sentence is somewhat odd in light of the last few lines of chapter 11. The Deity commands Abram to go "from your land, from the place where you were born, and from the house of your father" (12:1). As Fewell and Gunn point out, "Abram is to leave his native land which he has already done and his father's house, of which there is nothing left, to go to a land which is already the destination of his migration."[4] According to Gen 11:31, Abram's family is from Ur of the Chaldees, which he and his family have already left. One could question whether he has already left his father's house. If the text is referring to a physical house (in Ur), then the entire family, including his father, has apparently already left it. If the reference means the father's household (now in Haran), then a question is raised. According to Gen 11:32, the reader is led to believe that Abram's father is already dead, and thus leaving his household is not a big deal since there is no such thing, physical or metaphorical. Such is not the case since according to the age numbers in Genesis, Terah is alive for sixty years after Abram's departure (11:26, 32; 12:4). Finally, Abram's brother Haran has already done exactly the same thing (leaving his father's house), though in his case through death (11:28).

It is not clear if leaving his "father's house" includes leaving all the people associated with that house, or if Abram is allowed to take relatives along. This particularly concerns the inclusion of Lot, who appears again in the following line (12:4–5), and possibly his wife, Sarai. If leaving his father's house demands leaving his relatives, then the inclusion of Lot is problematic. Sarai is another issue. On the one hand she is his wife, and this author will later argue that there is no evidence in the text that they were anything other than spouses. Nevertheless, when speaking to Abimelech king of Gerar in Gen 20:12, Abraham claims that she is the daughter of his father, but not of his mother, and thus she could be considered part of his father's house.

The issue is not purely semantic. The text is trying to establish something new and yet is not prepared completely to sever it from everything previous. If the thrust of the text had been that Abraham was something completely new and was making a huge break, there would have been no need to spend so many verses in chapter 11 establishing Terah's connection to the line of Shem and Abram's relatives. Furthermore, if Abram was doing something radical in leaving his birthplace, then why did his father begin the journey toward Canaan (11:31)? The text obviously does not want Abram to make a complete break with his family: it spends a long chapter going through the details of how Abraham commissions his servant to find a wife for Isaac from his own family (Gen 24). Finally, if the promise points to the future generations and establishing family connections, it cannot begin by faulting those very connections.

One option often expressed in midrash is the notion that Abram's father was an idol maker or connected to idols in some way. This concept also appears in the book of Joshua, which that states that Terah "lived beyond the Euphrates and worshipped other gods" (Josh 24:2). There is no evidence of this concept in Genesis. If anything, Terah receives a rather favorable portrait, based on his position in the genealogy as part of the tenth generation after Noah, from the line of Shem, and the father of Abram.[5]

The Joshua reference also does not clarify questions concerning Abram's birthplace. In Gen 11:31, Abram and his family are from Ur of the Chaldees. The Joshua reference leaves open two possibilities when the Deity states, "I took your father Abraham from beyond the river" (Josh 24:3) since beyond the river Euphrates could be either Ur or Haran. In order for leaving Abram's birthplace to be a significant act in Gen 12:1, Haran must be considered his birthplace. Later, when Abraham seeks a wife for his son Isaac, he claims that he does not want his son to take a wife from the daughters of the Canaanites (24:4) and orders his servant to go to the place of his birth to find a wife. In that passage Abraham does not specifically name the land of his birth. The servant goes to Aram-Naharaim, to the city of Nahor (24:10), and Rebekah becomes the wife of Isaac, apparently to Abraham's satisfaction, though Abraham never comments on the servant's choice. One further complication is that the text does not list Nahor as joining the family on their trek to Haran with Terah in the first place. Thus, the reader is provided with two possible birthplaces for Abram.

Finally, the Deity adds that Abram should go "to the land that I will show you." Here the reader, and theoretically Abram, does not know that the intended place is precisely where Terah was going when he original-ly departed from Ur (11:31). The Deity also does not claim that Abram will receive the land.[6] The Deity simply states that the Deity will show Abram where to go, similar to the command in Gen 22:2 that the Deity will tell Abraham where in Moriah he should go when he is on his way to sacrifice his son Isaac (countermanded by the Deity; 22:11).

Readers traditionally count Abram's response in Gen 12 as indicating his tremendous faith and loyalty to the Deity (cf. 15:6; Heb 11:8); this is important for the story of Sarai. Speiser observes how Abram has to pull up stakes and make a complete break.[7] Von Rad hears the divine address as "the command to abandon radically all natural roots."[8] Yet, as discussed above, this is not precisely what the Deity requests. It is also true that Abram imposes the same response upon Sarai. In fact, one could easily argue that the same is demanded of all the matriarchs and is what Abram will later impose upon Ishmael (Gen 21:14).[9] We can even consider Abram's response a bit of dramatic foreshadowing: it is the scenario that a later exiled audience would possibly be experiencing in retrospect. The difference between Abram's actions to come and those just listed is one of choice, which only Abram has.

The next verse (12:2) highlights another difference between Abram and other foreshadowed experiences: the Deity promises to make Abram a large nation, bless him, make his name great (large), and make it become a blessing. The reference to making his name great ties immedi-ately to the tower of Babel. In that story, the people's goal for building the tower is "to make a name for ourselves else we be scattered all over the world" (11:4). In response, the Deity changes their speech so they cannot understand each other and scatters them over the face of the earth (11:6–8). The situation with Abram is somewhat ironic since the Deity is going to make his name great (similar terminology as 11:4), also by moving him. In both situations the Deity's intent seems to be on retaining control of who and what determines "greatness." In the Babel story the Deity keeps the people of Babel from creating their own greatness, and in the Abram story the Deity will create greatness for him.

The concept of "making one great" establishes the major promise to Abram. According to Turner, of all the promises to Abram the one that dominates the story implicitly and explicitly concerns Abram becoming a great nation.[10] If such is the case, the argument continues, then the issue that is uppermost in people's minds is that Sarai is a major obstacle to accomplishing this feat.[11] This means that while Sarai may not always be a major player in the story, from the very beginning of the focus on Abram, her status as his wife and as barren is a major factor of the plot, whether it is stated explicitly or not.

In the next verse Sarai does not appear, but what the Deity offers has great implications for what later happens to Sarai. Genesis 12:3 is traditionally translated, "I will bless those who bless you and curse him that curses you" (NJPS). On one level this is a legitimate translation; yet it avoids the differentiation in the nature of the cursing that is discussed because the text uses one verb for what people may do to Abram and another for the Deity's reaction. The first verb (what people may do to Abram) is from the root qof-lamed-lamed (qalal). The essence of the root translates "be slight, swift, trifling."[12] In this context it carries the connotation of "curse, make contemptible."[13] Those who carry out such action against their parents are subject to the penalty of death (Exod 21:17), and one is not allowed so to curse the deaf (Lev 19:14).

Harsh as this cursing action is, it is not as severe as the verb used for what the Deity will do to those who carry out that action: alef-resh-resh ('arar). This action is what Balak requests Balaam to do to the people of Israel (Num 22:6, 12). The example clearest and closest to this situation of what happens to someone who is cursed using this verb is in Gen 3:14 and 17. With this term ('arar) both the serpent and the ground are "cursed."

The severity of the human making a "curse" should not be taken lightly, though its force is less than the Deity's curse. A better translation might therefore be, "I will curse those who severely insult you." Since no one in Abram's family has yet been "severely insulted," the ramifications seem theoretical. In chapter 16, however, someone is "severely insulted," and thus 12:3 is important for understanding Sarai's later actions.

The next verse narrates what appears to be Abram's carrying out the Deity's request in the previous verse. In 12:4 Abram apparently follows the Deity's instructions. The verse also includes the note that Lot goes with him. The way the text conveys the information does not reveal whether Abram asks Lot to go or whether Lot asks to go. Again, the difference addresses the relationship between Lot and Abram. Is Abram the uncle taking care of his fatherless nephew, or is Lot choosing to go with Abram for reasons never stated by the text? The text suggests a major theme that Lot may be a potential heir to Abram because Sarai is barren, and then has Lot joining the clan in Canaan; both aspects are relevant. In fact, Turner argues that Abram considers Lot as his surrogate son and that therefore Abram understands the Deity's command about becoming a great nation as not coming necessarily through Sarai.[14] As narrated in 12:4, "and Lot went with him," Lot is the subject of the verb, possibly indicating that the decision is Lot's. The next verse complicates the situation by reversing the subject: Abram takes Lot. Again, if Abram takes Lot with him, he is not leaving all his family behind.[15]

In the following verse Sarai, clarified as Abram's wife, appears at the beginning of the list of all the things traveling with Abram from Haran to Canaan (12:5); they include Lot, identified as Abram's nephew; their possessions; and all the souls they had acquired. The previous verse mentions only Lot, with no discussion as to his relationship to Abram. Here 12:5 is specific about how both Sarai and Lot relate to Abram. In the previous verse Sarai does not appear, but here she is listed first. According to Steinberg, the absence of Sarai in 12:4, and her appearance first here along with the list and the nature of Sarai and Lot's relationships to Abram, underscore the fact that at this point Abram has no biological heirs.[16]

The verse also contains a list of other items traveling with them, including transportable goods and an odd reference to what appears to be people. This may possibly foreshadow later events concerning Jacob, who also leaves the same area with people and goods. One might argue that Laban later is correct to be expecting something like Jacob leaving with his children and flocks since that is precisely what Abram does earlier. What is the source of all these people and goods? While the text hints that Abram's father is dead, the text also states categorically that Abram is 75 at this point (12:4), and Terah therefore is still living. Does Abram take the people and the goods from his father? Is he taking his father's household?

The next three verses narrate Abram's movements upon arriving in the land. Abram arrives at Shechem, to the tree of Moreh (12:6); the Deity appears to him and offers the land to Abram's seed. After that, Abram builds an altar to the Deity, who appears to him. Then he travels to the hill east of Bethel, pitches his tent with Bethel on the west and Ai on the east, and builds another altar to the Deity. On the one hand it appears that upon arrival and completion of the Deity's command to leave Haran, Abram is rewarded with the promise of the land for Abram's seed. Again, readers are aware of Abram's lack of children. His reward will be received only by his descendants, whom he does not have at this point in the story; and because of Sarai's barren state, it appears that he will not have them through Sarai, his wife.

In Gen 12:9 Abram travels, in stages, to the Negev. In the biblical text the Negev refers to one of the main regions of Palestine, south of the hill country of Judah, west of the Arabah, and northeast of the Sinai peninsula.[17] The Hebrew word "Negev" means something like "dry south country."[18] It is on the way to Egypt and a place where Abram later in the story has encounters.[19] This move brings him closer to Egypt, where the next unit finds him. Genesis 12:9, combined with the lack of descendants raised with the previous verse (12:8), establishes the background necessary for understanding the story in Egypt, where Sarai and her relationship with Abram are highlighted.

Encounters in Egypt: Genesis 12:10–20

The episode in Egypt is extremely important to the rest of Israelite history. Abram and Sarai's visit is Israel's first contact with Egypt, which plays such a large part in the history of the people of Abram's descendants. It is also crucial for understanding the character of Sarai, her relationship to Abram and the Israelite Deity, and some of her later actions. The MT gives a significant break here, showing that the Masoretes consider this passage as a new topic. The text emphasizes the new topic by introducing news that there is a famine in the land. It still connects the event to the previous situation through the *vav* consecutive.

The episode begins with the narrator's comments that there is a famine in the land and Abram goes down to sojourn there (12:10). Scholars have given much discussion to Abram's departure from the land so early in the story and going to Egypt, of all places. Since the Deity commands Abram to go to the land that has just been shown to him, should he immediately leave that land? There are also a number of parallels between this story and Jacob and Joseph's entry into Egypt, which leads to the enslavement of the tribe/people, thus setting up the exodus story.[20] The text is careful to signal that Abram's stay in Egypt is only temporary by using the infinitive *lagur*, from *gimel-vav-resh* (*gur*), meaning, "to sojourn," rather than a word signaling an intention to stay for a long period of time.[21] The term carries with it the idea that the individual *ger* (sojourner, resident) is a temporary dweller and/or a newcomer.[22] Yet even a short stay leaves readers wondering about Abram's decision to go at all.[23] This is directly relevant to Sarai because it raises questions about the Abram's culpability in what happens to Sarai even before his conversation with her.

Upon the couple's approach to Egypt, Abram says something about Sarai's beauty (12:11). The line is usually translated as a straightforward comment, with Abram stating that he knows his wife is beautiful (LXX, KJV, RSV, NJPS). But the conversation is more complicated than these translations suggest, with much greater meaning to the verse and the story at large. Speiser raises the question as to who knows about Sarai's looks since the verb *yada'ti* (I know) can be the simple first person masculine singular perfect of "know," or it could be an archaic form of the second feminine singular "you know."[24] The "compliment" Abram gives to Sarai about her looks is not a straightforward "beautiful," as the Egyptians will later claim (12:14), but "beautiful of appearance" (*y'fat-mar'eh*). This is not surprising since Abram refers to Sarai's looks while explaining what actions he thinks they should take as a result of this reality. Van Dijk recognizes that the comment on Sarai's beauty is not an utterance of joy that might evoke a similar reaction from Sarai, nor a dialogue between lovers (like Song 1:15–16), but a statement of potential risk.[25] That Abram views Sarai's beauty as negative is clear not only by his later actions but also by the phrase he uses to refer to it: "beautiful of appearance."

Another element often lost in translations is how Abram begins to ask the question. In 12:11 he uses the phrase *hinneh-na'*, which can mean "behold, please," but is seldom translated in this verse.[26] The problem involves the particle *na'*, which may or may not translate well with a word. *Hinneh* is usually translated as a demonstrative particle, "Lo! Behold!" and takes an accusative noun or pronoun.[27] Generally the word introduces clauses involving predication.[28] When a proposal is to be an entreaty or a request, *hinneh-na'* is often used.[29] Another way of expressing an entreaty in a polite form is the English word "please," by which the term *na'* is translated in certain circumstances. While the precise wording here may be difficult, the Hebrew terminology conveys the concept that Abram is trying to entreat Sarai or at least ask her nicely.[30] He knows he is asking something of someone who can control his future, and he expresses that through the language he employs. The terminology he uses to refer to her beauty and the structure of the sentence all communicate that he is not offering a mere compliment but is about to ask something rather significant of his wife.

The next three verses establish a great deal about Abram and Sarai's relationship, though there are a few ways of understanding precisely the implications of his intent. They are the first of the wife-sister stories in Genesis, something about which a great deal has been written.[31] The present discussion is focused on the character of Sarai, and therefore we will examine the story in light of the way it appears at this point in the story without regard to trends, redactional history, or parallels from Nuzi. In Gen 12:12 Abram continues to speak to Sarai, reasoning that, because of her beauty, the Egyptians will see her, kill him, and let her live. The next verse presents his proposed resolution to the problem: she should say that she is his sister, so that things will "go well for him through her" and he will remain alive through her (12:13).

Does Abram really believe the story he tells Sarai? Traditionally, this question is not asked despite the fact that the issue only dawns on Abram once they are at the doorstep of Egypt; Abram did not seem to be concerned about this danger when he decided to travel to Egypt in the first place.[32] Most assume that Abram feared for his life, and that the only way to save it is through a little white lie. Abram is at risk to the "vicissitudes of nature and the whims of an alien society in which he unwillingly finds himself."[33] Because of the role of the brother in the ancient Near East, Abram is in a position to control what happens to Sarai.[34] The fact that Pharaoh's courtiers take Sarai then serves as proof that Abram's fears were legitimate. Foreshadowing is even a factor since later when the sons of Israel are in Egypt, it is the men who are at risk, not the women (Exod 1:16, 22).[35]

The problem with Abram's story is that while the courtiers later take Sarai, their actions are based on the notion that Abram and Sarai are brother and sister (Gen 12:19) and that Sarai therefore is an unmarried woman. There is no extrabiblical evidence from the ancient Near East that husbands were killed so that kings could marry their wives. There is only one such case in the biblical text: King David has Uriah the Hittite "die in battle" so that he may marry Uriah's wife, Bathsheba, whom David has already impregnated (2 Sam 11). Is this foreshadowing? Are Abram's concerns legitimate, or is he trying to get rid of his barren wife so that he can have children, thereby actualizing the Deity's promise?

While this last option may be taking the case too far, I raise it here as a question because of the way this passage depicts Abram. He is not afraid to leave his home and his family because the Deity asks him to do so. Abram faces a famine, and his faith does not convince him to stay in the land. Instead, he travels to a land where he could be killed because of his wife's beauty. Why is it more legitimate to go to Egypt and enter such danger rather than going back home for a short while? With his wife in another man's house, who would produce heirs to fulfill the Deity's promise? Since the use of the term *ger* earlier (Gen 12:10) suggests that he was not planning on residing in Egypt for a long term, did he expect the Egyptians to return his wife to him? Or do scholars traditionally not raise these questions about Abram because "within an interpretive community that views the patriarchs as paragons of virtue and their life-narratives as edifying instructions to future generations such ambiguity cannot be tolerated. Jewish and Christian exegetes throughout the ages have focused most of their interpretive efforts on dispelling these ambiguities in their realistic reading of the text."[36]

Precisely how Abram words his request is relevant. One possible translation of 12:13 is, "Please say you are my sister so that it will be good for me because of you and my 'soul' will live because of you." Once again, Abram entreats Sarai, using *na'*, meaning "please" (as in NASB, NKJV) or "I pray thee" (KJV, BDB), though many versions skip this word. Though he claims that he will live because of her, it is not his first comment. He seems to have great insight into the Egyptians' culture by first stating that it will be good for him because of her. Later, 12:16 reports that "because of her it went well with Abram; he acquired sheep, oxen, asses, male and female slaves, she-asses, and camels." Abram becomes rich because of Sarai. Since this comes true, Abram could be considered clever, figuring out the game in advance. Yet because the story tells of Abram's acquisition of wealth *before* the saving of his life (12:19–20), one can speculate as to how concerned he was about his life versus gaining wealth.

Abram asks Sarai nicely to say she is his sister, and claims it is to save his life; but nowhere does he explain what might happen to her by pretending she is not married. Does she even realize the danger she could be in by claiming to be his sister? As will be the case for this entire unit, Sarai has no response. In later chapters she speaks, but here in the narrative the reader learns nothing of her feelings, reactions to Abram's request, or her time in Pharaoh's household.

Upon Abram and Sarai's entry to Egypt, Pharaoh's courtiers notice Sarai's beauty and praise her to Pharaoh, so she is taken to Pharaoh's palace (12:14–15). The result is that things go well financially for Abram (12:16). It is not completely clear precisely what happens to Sarai and how Abram benefits from the situation.

The text is playful with the words used here, particularly in verse 15. To begin with, the word usually translated as "courtiers" is *sarei* and, while pointed and therefore vocalized differently, contains the same consonants as Sarai's name. The Egyptians see the *'ishah*, usually translated as "woman." But in Hebrew this one word means "woman" and/or "wife"; thus, while the courtiers see a woman, they are also seeing a wife. It is a case where both meanings of the word should be understood as functioning at the same time. The text also says that "she was taken" to Pharaoh's palace, employing the passive. The root used is *laqach*, which in an active sense means "to take," but also often with sexual connotations, as "to take in marriage."[37] In the later story, where Abraham gives his wife, Sarah, to Abimelech of Gerar, the text states categorically that the foreign king did not know her sexually (20:4). The text adds no such comment here.

The role of Sarai in Pharaoh's house relates to how Abram does well in Egypt "on account of" Sarai. One option is that she is in Pharaoh's harem, and therefore Abram has access to things otherwise not available to him. Another is that she is considered a wife of the Pharaoh, meaning that the Egyptians count him as a brother-in-law of sorts to the Pharaoh, one who maybe even negotiated her marriage.[38] The precise meaning of the words may help. According to van Dijk-Hemmes the preposition usually translated "on account of"—with the object "you" (*ba'aburekh*) in 12:13 or "her" (*ba'aburah*) in 12:16—should be rendered "for the price of (you/her)," as in Amos 2:6 and 8:6.[39] Based on the grammar of the verse, van Dijk-Hemmes interprets that Abram sells/arranges a marriage or barters for her. What is clear is that Abram blames her for his life being at risk, and his resolution is to give her, most likely sexually, to another man so that he will both live and prosper financially.[40] From what the text has provided thus far, in Abram's plan there is no exit strategy for Sarai from Pharaoh's house or any foreseeable reunification with Abram.

The Israelite Deity instigates a resolution to the situation. The text reports that the Israelite Deity afflicts Pharaoh and his household with "great plagues" because of Sarai, Abram's wife. The text uses powerful language, foreshadowing the later exodus from Egypt by using the same word for "plague" (*nega'*) that labels the last plague in Egypt, the slaying of the firstborn (Exod 11:1).[41] The narrator is explicit that this is because of the *d'var* of Sarai. *D'var* can mean "speech/word" or, as more suitable here, "matter/affair."[42] While the precise translation leaves open a number of options, all of them explicitly state that the Deity takes action because of (the affair of) Sarai, not Abram. This is the first of many situations where the Deity comes to Sarai's aid because of situations in which Abram has placed her.

Pharaoh's reaction indicates that Abram's original premise, that he would be killed so that the Egyptians or Pharaoh could take Sarai, may not have been true. Pharaoh also clarifies who originally described the couple's relationship. He sends for Abram and says to him, "What have you done to me? Why did you not tell me that she was your wife? Why did you say, 'she is my sister,' so that I took her as my wife?" (12:18–19). While it is easy to question Pharaoh's sincerity, as Jeansonne comments, when Pharaoh remonstrates against Abram, he does not mention the harshness of the plagues but stresses the wrongness of Abram's actions.[43] Pharaoh actually confronts Abram in the same manner, "What have you done?" that the Deity uses with Adam and Eve (3:13) and Cain (4:10) after their transgressions.[44] In this case, Abram remains silent.

Pharaoh no longer wants anything to do with the couple and tells Abram to take his wife and go. He wants Abram to leave so badly that he puts men in charge of him and sends him off with his wife and all his possessions (12:20). As a result of the events in Egypt, Abram leaves with his wife and a great deal of wealth. There is no more discussion about a famine in the land. Whether or not the famine ends does not matter since the couple is banished from Egypt, their supposed refuge.

Genesis 13: Abram and Lot and the Land

According to most translations the following verse begins a new chapter since the customary division of chapter and verse has a new chapter beginning with Gen 13:1. However, the MT has no such break here, and the following verses continue the preceding story. The problem with the break is evident in that commentaries differ as to where to begin and end the unit. Most see 13:1 as ending the episode in Egypt, with the following verses narrating the conflict between Abram and Lot concerning their numerous flocks. Yet if there is no break (before or after 13:1), then one must understand the contents of chapter 13 as somehow tied to the episode in Egypt, something that is considered here. This is especially relevant since 12:1–9 refers to both Sarai and Lot, and 12:10–20 focuses primarily on Sarai. In Gen 13, Sarai disappears and Lot reappears.

Where Is Lot?

Many of the differences regarding a break before or after 13:1 surround Lot's presence or absence in Egypt. Chapter 13 begins by reporting that "Abram went up from Egypt," clarifying the party as "he and his wife and all that he had," and then says that Lot traveled with him toward the Negev (13:1). So, where is Lot when Abram is in Egypt? If Lot also is in Egypt, there is a peculiar silence about that which ends as soon as Abram leaves Egypt. Another possible reading is that Lot does not go down to Egypt with him. The theological ramifications of that are rather significant: it would mean that Lot stays in the land despite the famine and still manages to prosper financially. Further support for that notion is that the conflict between Abram and Lot's people only arises when they leave Egypt, raising the possibility that there is no conflict in Egypt because they are not there together. There is no reference to the source of Lot's wealth, but the text is quite specific that Abram became wealthy in Egypt because of Sarai (12:16).

Few commentators discuss the difference, and their dealings with it reveals how the placement of the beginning of the story impacts the situation. Brueggemann keeps 12:10–13:18 as one unit but sees a major break beginning with 13:1.[45] He highlights the juxtaposition of the two units: "Both texts, 12:10–20 and 13:1–18, are illuminated by placing them in tension. It is the relation between the two which poses the hard issues of faith."[46] While he understands that 12:10–20 should be read together, he still understands the beginning of 13:1 as a fundamental shift.

Speiser begins a new section with 13:1, claiming chapter 13 is about Abram's generosity. Chapter 12 is about wife-sister issues, establishing the superior strain of the line, and the importance of purity in the mother's line.[47] Von Rad deals with the theological issues of Lot not being in Egypt by making 13:1 the last verse of the unit in Egypt.[48] By placing 13:1, where the text says that Abram and Lot travel through the Negev together, as the end of the episode in Egypt, Lot becomes part of the

Egyptian experience. His placement of 13:1 obscures any question as to Lot's whereabouts.

Nevertheless, despite the previous commentators, the text does not state that Lot is with the couple in Egypt. Further doubt as to Lot's presence in Egypt is that Abram and Lot have different things when they meet in the Negev: Abram is rich in flocks, silver, and gold (13:3), while Lot has flocks, herds, and tents (13:5).

Purpose of Genesis 13

The rest of chapter 13 focuses on the conflict between Abram and Lot's herdsmen, and its resolution by Abram giving Lot the choice of land. Traditional approaches focus on how, though the Deity promises the land to Abram's descendants, Abram is a loving uncle by giving Lot first choice of the land. Proof of this is the Deity's reaction by being more specific about the land originally offered, and by giving it directly to Abram (13:15). Previously the Deity offered the land only to Abram's offspring (12:7), which he does not have by this point in the narrative. Other ways of viewing elements of the chapter may not necessarily concern Sarai but focus on Abram's relationship with the Deity and his faithfulness to the Deity's commands.

It is not clear that Lot left the land to go to Egypt with Abram and Sarai. If Lot does not leave the land of Canaan, his original "rights" to the land, or at least his impression of those rights, may be different from Abram's. Many have noticed Abram's devotion to the Deity by returning to the place where he originally established an altar (13:3). Yet if his leaving the land in the first place is problematic, then reestablishing his connection to the Deity and the land should be a primary concern, especially in front of Lot.

Commentators make much of Abram's offer for Lot to choose the land in which he will dwell. As Brueggeman says: "In chapter 13, Abraham is very different. He takes no thought of himself."[49] In chapter 13 Abram is completely selfless, but in chapter 12 he sacrifices his wife for himself. The contrast is striking and will not be the last time that two stories concerning Abram and others reveal a selfless Abram in relation to anyone other than his wife, Sarai.

There also are other problems concerning Abram's offer. While the Deity promises the land to Abram's offspring (12:7), in the early part of chapter 13 Abram has no descendants, and therefore the land is not yet his. The text reinforces this status: "The Canaanites and Perizzites were then dwelling in the land" (13:7). Thus, while there is a divine promise to Abram and his descendants, at this point theoretical, fulfillment of the promise has not yet occurred.

Possibly more troubling is whether the land is Abram's to offer. The Deity promises the land to Abram's descendants, and Abram immediately leaves the land. Upon his return he first goes back to the place where the land is promised to his descendants, and he gives it to someone else, his nephew. It turns out that Lot makes a bad choice, as will become clear in the next chapter, but does it legitimate Abram's offer? Readers usually consider Lot selfish for choosing the "good-looking land," and reckon his choice as outside of the land of Canaan, further proof that Lot makes bad decisions.[50] Yet the land that Lot chooses, according to the text, was previously defined as the border of Canaan (10:19) and possibly included in the Deity's original offer to Abram.

Conclusions

Chapter 13 focuses on Abram and Lot. Sarai does not appear after verse 1, and yet the chapter is relevant for what it says about Abram. The text gives no indication that Lot is with Abram and Sarai in Egypt—thus raising questions about the necessity for the couple to leave the land. When they are reunited with Lot, Lot also is wealthy, and therefore Abram is solicitous of him. By offering Lot land that does not belong to Abram but to his future descendants, Abram treats Lot far kinder than he recently treated his own wife in Egypt. As a result, the MT's structure of maintaining 12:10–13:18 as one unit preserves many issues lost when they are separated.

In these chapters Sarai appears as the one Abram treats the worst in his extended family. Abram knows that he is asking something significant of her, since all indications are that he expected her to be taken into Pharaoh's harem. His concern is not with her but for his own life and wealth. The source of Abram's magnitude toward Lot is not clear: familial ties, potential heir, or wealthy neighbor? In any case the juxtaposition is clear: Abram takes care of Lot. On the other hand Sarai is a liability, and Abram uses her best to support his goals and aspirations.

One point often lost in the discussion is the role of the Deity. The Deity saves Sarai in Egypt and will save her again. While Abram may not have much use for her, the Israelite Deity does, taking actions repeatedly on her behalf.

Notes

1. See the discussion in the preceding chapter.

2. In the Jewish tradition the Pentateuch is broken up into *parashot*, "weekly readings," so that the entire Pentateuch is covered during the Jewish year; first and last readings fall on the holiday of Simchat Torah (*simkhat torah*).

3. The NJPS reads "Go forth," while the RSV translates simply "Go."

4. D. Fewell and D. Gunn, *Gender Power and Promise: The Subject of the Bible's First Story* (Nashville: Abingdon, 1993), 40.

5. Noah was the tenth generation of the line of Seth after Noah, and the text names him a "righteous man, blameless in his age" (Gen 6:9 NJPS), though everything is relative.

6. The Deity's promise to give Abram the land does not really come until Gen 13:15 and 15:7.

7. E. A. Speiser, *Genesis* (Anchor Bible 1; Garden City, N.Y.: Doubleday, 1985), 87.

8. G. von Rad, *Genesis: A Commentary* (Old Testament Library; Philadelphia: Westminster, 1972), 159.

9. Genesis 21 does not create a break for Hagar from "natural roots" because she has earlier been forced to leave her country and family in servitude (13:1); she returns to Egypt to get a wife for her son (21:21).

10. L. A. Turner, *Announcement of Plot in Genesis* (JSOTSup 96; Sheffield: JSOT Press, 1990), 61.

11. Ibid.

12. See BDB, 886.

13. Ibid.

14. Turner, *Announcement of Plot*, 63.

15. Ibid., 62.

16. N. Steinberg, *Kinship and Marriage in Genesis: A Household Economics Perspective* (Minneapolis: Fortress, 1993), 50.

17. S. A. Rosen, "Negeb," *ABD* 4:1061.

18. Ibid.

19. With Abimelech (Gen 20; 21:22–34), and specifically the area of Beer-sheba (22:19).

20. S. Pace Jeansonne, *The Women of Genesis: From Sarah to Potiphar's Wife* (Minneapolis: Fortress, 1990), 16. According to Jeansonne, from the choice of locale and language, the narrator builds toward the famine in Joseph's day and later Israelite residence in Egypt. This event also foreshadows Joseph's brothers going down, which is the beginning of the exodus/Egypt cycle.

21. BDB, 158.

22. Ibid.

23. Some interpreters take a severe view of Abram's action of going down to Egypt; for example, W. Brueggemann, *Genesis* (Interpretation; Atlanta: John Knox, 1982), 127, comments: "12:10–20, quite in contrast to 12:1–9, presents Abraham as an anxious man, a man of unfaith."

24. Speiser, *Genesis*, 90, says that "I know" normally is first person perfect. The Samaritan Pentateuch has *'ty*, meaning that it is archaic second person "you know," which he claims would suit the context, though in his translation he employs "I know."

25. F. van Dijk-Hemmes, "Sarai's Exile: A Gender-Motivated Reading of Genesis 12:10–13:2," in *A Feminist Companion to Genesis 2* (ed. A. Brenner; Sheffield: Sheffield Academic Press, 1997), 227.

26. The RSV, NJPS, and LXX do not translate the particle *na'* for 12:11, though NJPS does for 12:13.

27. BDB, 243–44.

28. Ibid.

29. Ibid.

30. The examples used to convey this concept in BDB are Gen 12:11; 16:2; 18:27; 1 Kgs 20:31; 22:13. Though NJPS uses no device to convey the sense of the phrase in this particular context, it will be translated in Gen 12:13.

31. Rather than list the traditional sources that focus on these issues, I am including one with a full bibliography on the issues, also a critique of them, and another approach to considering the three incidents: J. C. Exum, "Who's Afraid of 'The Endangered Ancestress'?" in *Women in the Hebrew Bible: A Reader* (ed. A. Bach; New York: Routledge, 1999), 141–56.

32. F. van Dijk-Hemmes, "Sarai's Exile," 228.

33. Barry Eichler, "On Reading Genesis 12:10–20," in *Tehillah le-Moshe: Biblical and Judaic Studies in Honor of Moshe Greenberg* (ed. Mordechai Cogan, Barry L. Eichler, and Jeffrey H. Tigay; Winona Lake: Eisenbrauns, 1997), 27.

34. Ibid.

35. According to van Dijk-Hemmes, "Sarai's Exile," 228, there is a difference between men and women, as in the later threat in Exod 1, since foreign sons are considered a threat; foreign daughters are different because they can be "taken" and incorporated into one's own people.

36. Eichler, "On Reading Genesis 12:10–20," 28.

37. BDB, 542–44.

38. Eichler, "On Reading Genesis 12:10–20," 37–38.

39. Van Dijk-Hemmes, "Sarai's Exile," 22.

40. On some level, one could see this as Abram selling Sarah into slavery, something that was not uncommon in the ancient Near East. Slavery in the ancient Near East was complex (see discussion on Gen 16:1, pages 46–53). Unfortunately, most of our information about ancient laws regulating slavery came from Mesopotamia, not Egypt.

41. BDB, 619.

42. Ibid., 182–83.

43. S. Pace Jeansonne, *The Women of Genesis*, 17.

44. F. V. Greifenhagen, *Egypt on the Pentateuch's Ideological Map: Constructing Biblical Israel's Identity* (JSOTSup 361; London: Sheffield Academic Press, 2002), 29.

45. Brueggemann, *Genesis*, 125.

46. Ibid., 132.
47. Speiser, *Genesis*, 93–94 (on Gen. 12), 97–98 (on Gen 13).
48. Von Rad, *Genesis*, 167.
49. Brueggemann, *Genesis*, 133.
50. C. Westermann, *Genesis 12–36* (Minneapolis: Augsburg, 1985), 177.

CHAPTER 3

Changing Status: Genesis 14–17

Genesis 16 is one of the most crucial chapters for understanding the role of Sarai in the text. Here she has her first dealings with her servant Hagar that lead to the birth of Ishmael, an incident for which she is severely taken to task in much of the later literature. Yet in order to understand Sarai's actions in Gen 16, we must consider what happens to her in 12:10–20. Gen 16 is usually disassociated from the previous chapters, as though nothing has happened in the development of her husband and his role and stature in the area or in his relationship with the Deity. It is also seldom discussed in connection with the following chapter, Gen 17, where Sarah is named as the person who will be the mother of nations. This study will reveal how relevant the surrounding material is for understanding Sarai by reviewing some of the highlights from Gen 14–15 before focusing on Gen 16 and tying Gen 16 to Gen 17.

Abram, Regional Politics, and the Covenant: Genesis 14–15

The text of Genesis flows neatly from the end of Gen 12 to Gen 15 through the character of Lot. Despite modern divisions of the text at the end of Gen 12, the Masoretes and many other scholars have trouble separating the end of the episode in Egypt from the beginning of the conflict between Abram and Lot's herdsman. Gen 13 reminds the reader of the presence of Lot in the area and his role in the family dynamic. His depar-

42

ture to the Transjordan establishes his presence in that region, setting up the context for Abram's entry into regional and international politics.

Chapter 14 recounts the machinations of what are apparently foreign entities exercising some form of political power in the Transjordan. In the view of most scholars, "the most enigmatic chapter in Genesis, chapter 14 seems to stand utterly alone and without connection to any of the sources or strands of tradition found elsewhere in the book."[1] What seems clear to most is that the flow from Gen 13–15 focuses on Lot and the repercussions of his actions in Gen 13. One of the main reasons for the confusion about chapter 14 and its role surrounds its "historicity": when and where does one place the various kings and nations involved? Thus, the emphasis in most commentaries is on determining the source, date, and possible identities of the characters in the chapter.[2] What is relevant for this discussion is not so much who the kings are and when to date them, but what the impact of the episode is on the characters who are the focus of this study: Abram, Sarai, and to some extent, Lot.

A general review of the chapter should suffice to highlight what happens to the characters here, though Sarai is not named. Lot moves to a place that has a history of turmoil involving some nations, clearly depicted in the text as "foreign" since they are not from regionally known locales but places such as Shinar,[3] Ellasar,[4] Elam,[5] and Goiim (14:1).[6] These wars take Lot away, along with the wealth of Sodom (14:11–12). Abram hears a report of what happened and immediately musters a group of people born in his household. Precisely who or what these people are is complicated since the term used to refer to these individuals is a hapax legomenon, not appearing anywhere else in the biblical text.[7] Whatever its precise translation, the men seem to be in Abram's control and have military capabilities, a fairly large contingent of 318. The text has not mentioned many numbers thus far in Genesis. If Abram has 318 armed men with him, this might be a good explanation for why Lot and Abram could not continue together. Abram and his company are strong enough to attack at night, defeat, and pursue this foreign element as far as Hobah, defined by the text as north of Damascus (14:15), bringing back all the possessions and Lot (14:16). Since this is the only reference to Hobah in the Hebrew Bible, it is difficult to determine precisely where or if this was a site in antiquity.[8]

In a mere three verses, the text reports the events from Abram hearing of Lot's capture to his recovery of Lot and the defeat of the foreign army; this indicates that the battle with the foreign army is not the main interest of the incident. In fact, nine verses describe the history of the conflict

and the participants, and another two recount the escape of the kings of
Sodom and Gomorrah and the capture of Lot. The focus of the text
therefore is elsewhere. Examining what the episode does to the character
of Abram may hold the key to what is the interest of the text.

Prior to this report Abram is an immigrant with no family, sent to a
foreign land by his Deity (12:1). In Gen 12:10 he describes himself as at
the mercy of the Egyptian Pharaoh's libido because of his wife, justifying
why he gives her over to Pharaoh (12:12). He does well financially but is
exiled from Egypt because of his apparent lie to the Pharaoh about his
relationship with Sarai, communicated to the Pharaoh only through the
intervention of the Deity (12:19–20). When Abram leaves Egypt and
enters the land of Canaan again, he has too many flocks to stay with Lot.
Suddenly in Gen 14, Abram has the ability to mobilize a force of 318 men
born into his own household and defeat a major army of foreign kings, a
force that even the local governments combined could not defeat for fourteen years. Abram and his status in the region have changed radically.

Proof of this is found at the end of the chapter; King Melchizedek of
Salem comes out to bless Abram in the name of *El Elyon* (*'el 'elyon*, "God
Most High," 14:18). Most translations then report that Abram gave
Melchizedek a "tenth of everything,"[9] thus establishing Abram's recogni-
tion of the role of Salem and foreshadowing the role that Salem, possibly
Jerusalem, will have (14:19; cf. Ps 76:2). What commentators do not usu-
ally emphasize is that the previous verse mentions the king of Sodom as
the first local ruler coming out to meet Abram, at the King's Valley (near
Jerusalem; cf. 2 Sam 18:18; Gen 15:17). Melchizedek and the king of
Sodom thus carry out similar actions. Following Melchizedek's act of
blessing, Abram's name (14:20) must be inserted into the text in order for
Abram to be the subject of the sentence and the one tithing.[10] The
assumption seems to be that since, in the next verse, Abram rejects resti-
tution from the king of Sodom (14:21), the person offering a tithe here
must be Abram. Yet in light of what Abram has just accomplished, free-
ing the region from foreign rule, the king of Salem might be making an
offering/bribe to Abram, clearly a new force to be reckoned with in the
region. It is unclear what the motivation would be for Abram to offer
something to the king of Salem, whom Abram has just met, perhaps for
the first time. Abram is a resident alien since he identifies himself as such
when Sarah dies in Gen 23:4. Abram tithing to Melchizedek would be
giving funds to another Deity and/or local king since, according to the
text, Melchizedek is a king and adherent of *El Elyon*. Though a few vers-

es later Abram assimilates the reference to *El Elyon* into a reference to his own Deity (14:22), such has not yet happened in 14:20.

Another reason to support the notion that Melchizedek gives tithes to Abram is that in the next verse the king of Sodom offers Abram something quite different. The king of Sodom, who has run away in the battle (14:10), offers Abram all the possessions that Abram recovered (14:21). Abram rejects the offer because he does not want people to say that the king of Sodom made him rich (14:23)—though it is fine to Abram (but not to the Deity; 12:17) that he has offered his wife to Pharaoh of Egypt to make him that way. Yet he does let the men who were with him take their share, thereby garnering more loyalty from his own troops (14:24). Finally, if Abram were the one giving a tenth of everything to Melchizedek, it is not clear that what Abram is offering is what he already has or what he takes from the battle. In other words, if Abram were the one tithing, it appears that he is giving Melchizedek a tenth of what he recovers for the king of Sodom, the very thing he refuses to accept in the following verses.

The chapter can be summarized as Abram racing to the rescue of Lot, his nephew, to battle against foreign enemies, and refusing to accept payment for this from the king who should have protected his people. Abram does all this because he wants the people in the region to view him as a self-made man. Observe the contrast with the man so in fear of Pharaoh that he lies about his relationship to his wife and lets the Egyptians take her into Pharaoh's harem while he prospers financially. One may ask, especially in light of the tower of Babel incident: Is Abram supposed to consider himself a self-made man, a "wife-made man," or should he claim to be a "Deity-made" man?[11]

The timing between the end of Gen 14 and 15 is not clear. Genesis 15 reports what happened "sometime later" (15:1). Regardless of how much time has passed, it is clearly after the incidents recorded in Gen 14, and the new Abram seems to have a different relationship with the Israelite Deity as well. The Deity begins by telling Abram not to fear since his reward will be great. Rather than the supposedly docile Abram of Gen 12, who follows the Deity's orders immediately (or does he? See above), this Abram does not automatically accept what his Deity has to say. Instead, he questions the Deity's comments by asking what the Deity can do for him since he does not have an heir. In this case, the Deity states categorically that Abram's heir will be one of his own issue (15:4), though not specifying a mother. In Gen 15:2, Abram claims that some Eliezer will be his heir. This is an odd statement, since there is no previous reference to this person and their position is not qualified other than being "in charge of my house." The reference implies that Abram's nephew Lot either is no longer, or never was, a potential heir. Following so closely on Gen 13–14, where Lot chooses Sodom and Abram must then save both Lot and Sodom, this could mean that Lot's poor decision led Abram to dismiss Lot as an heir. Another possibility is that Lot never was a potential heir and the hints to his status as such were literary devices to build the drama of the story. The Deity then shows Abram the stars and tells him that Abram's offspring will likewise be uncountable (15:5). The next verse is usually considered proof that Abram was a man of faith because he put his trust in the Deity, who reckoned it to his merit (15:6). This understanding of Abram is not completely correct because Abram immediately demands proof (15:8). The result is a sacrifice. The Deity then designates the land that will be given to Abram's descendants with more clarity than previously, defining it as stretching from the Brook/River of Egypt to the Euphrates (15:20).[12]

The result of Gen 14 and 15 is a new Abram. He is not afraid of foreign or local kings, and he controls his own army. He also no longer seems to fear his own Deity in the same way. In Gen 12 Abram needs no evidence of the Deity's plans; now he questions what the Deity can do for him and insists on proof.

Sarai and Hagar: Genesis 16:1–6

It is to this new Abram that Sarai offers Hagar. Commentators usually treat Gen 16 as a new topic completely divorced from the previous three chapters in terms of content and players. They do not consider the change in Abram's character relevant since they relegate the chapters to "different sources" and sideline the ramifications of those changes on the family dynamics. Yet that approach ignores the character development of Abram, some of the motivation of Sarai, and what the role of Hagar's son means for the entire group. In the beginning of Gen 16 Sarai takes charge of Abram's lack-of-offspring situation, which could be considered resolved favorably by the end of the chapter when Abram receives his son Ishmael. The whole saga is complex, and the issues surrounding Abram's son and the roles of the various individuals involved in his birth raise issues that will plague Abram's family for chapters to come.

Genesis 16 begins with defining Sarai as Abram's wife, who has borne him no children.[13] The verse continues by reporting that Sarai has an Egyptian female maid named Hagar. Both of these comments establish the issue from the beginning: Abram's lack of children from his wife, and a slave-girl with the potential of fertility.

The verse establishes Hagar's status. The text defines her as Sarai's Egyptian *shifchah* (16:1). The first element of the verse is clear: Hagar belongs to Sarai. The second element is packed with meaning: Hagar is Egyptian. Egypt is not only foreign but is the place of Sarai's previous enslavement, where she learned that women can be sold to protect the lives of family members and make them rich regardless of the impact on the woman. Gen 12:16 and 13:2 list what Abram receives when he is in Egypt, and there is no information for the Egyptian episode that Sarai receives anything. The reference to Hagar as Egyptian and belonging to Sarai would be the only indication that she receives anything from her time in Egypt, though the text does not state it so categorically. The third element in Hagar's introduction is slightly problematic. She is labeled a *shifchah*, a term that has been variously translated as handmaid, maid, or maidservant.[14] The precise role of these women is not readily apparent, but both in this case and later with the wives of Jacob, the women are given female slaves, whom they later offer for procreative purposes to their spouses (29:24, 29; 30:1–12). This one verse identifies the relationship of Sarai to Abram and Hagar, and establishes the groundwork for Sarai's plan (16:1).

In Gen 16:2 Sarai suggests to Abram that the Deity has kept her from bearing and asks him please to consort with her maid so that she shall have a son through her. Sarai uses the term *na'* before she says that the Deity has kept her from bearing. In Gen 12, the precise meaning of *na'* is not always easily translated, though it usually indicates some sort of entreaty. Here, Sarai entreats Abram, and the text uses language to show that to be the case. Many translators, such as NJPS, von Rad, and Speiser, make no reference to the signs of entreaty. While some may argue that the difference is minor, the reality is that deleting the two references to "please" in 16:2 changes Sarai's request into a command. By deleting any reference to an entreaty, the text reads as though Sarai were commanding Abram to do something rather than asking him deferentially. This difference significantly affects the interpretation of Sarai's character. Rather than demanding something from Abram, as the text reads without translating the term "please," Sarai is asking something significant of him, just as Abram did of Sarai in Egypt (12:13). Deleting the sign of entreaty from the text is an example of interpreting the text in the translation process. By turning Sarai's request into a command, she becomes demanding rather than deferential.

The terminology used in Gen 16:2 contains a number of different nuances in the Hebrew due to the wordplay. The text literally states that she wants Abram to consort with Hagar so that she will "be built up" through her. But the term "to be built up" ('*ibaneh*) is the same as "to become the mother of a son/child,"[15] and thus she is asking for both a son and some sort of status. Because Sarai's request can be understood on different levels, there is a fair amount of discussion about what she is asking and the legitimacy of her request. Brueggemann claims that, theologically, Sarai's request reveals that she does not trust the promise.[16] Trible establishes Sarai as privileged and goes on to say that Sarai's offer of Hagar makes Hagar "one of the first females in scripture to experience use, abuse and rejection."[17]

Yet, are Sarai's actions really so bad? Exum points out that Sarai is asking Abram to do what already happens to Sarai in Egypt.[18] Contrary to claims that Sarai and her spouse are acting outside the bounds of faith, there is nothing in Sarai's plan that counters anything promised by the Deity in Gen 15. In that chapter the Deity offers Abram progeny of his own issue (15:4), with no comment about the role Sarai would play in the birth of an heir. In fact, in light of how Abram has treated Sarai thus far in the narrative, selling her in Egypt in contrast to rushing off to save Lot, becoming a major player in regional politics—it would be in Sarai's best interests to be involved in procuring progeny for Abram, in an effort to retain some status in the family. Finally, as Steinberg points out, Sarai's plan will meet with divine approval.[19]

Abram clearly has no trouble with Sarai's plan and promptly heeds her request (16:2). In 16:3 the text is again specific about everyone's relationship to each other when it reports that Sarai, defined as Abram's wife, takes her maid, again clarified as Hagar and Egyptian, and gives her to her husband. The text also adds, following the description of Hagar as Egyptian, that this occurs after Abram has lived in the land of Canaan for ten years, thus with no time off for his Egyptian sojourn (age 75 [12:4], 85 [16:3], 86 [16:16]).

The reference to the triangular relationships is particularly powerful because a shift in status may take place for Hagar. The end of 16:3 states that Abram takes the woman as a woman/wife. While some translations include this reference, NJPS, Speiser, and others have trouble with the concept and translate "as concubine" instead of "as wife."[20] The implications of Sarai's actions are often lost because of what follows. Yet, before we consider what follows, we should evaluate Sarai's action on its own merit without assuming knowledge of the whole story—something readers have but not the characters.

Sarai offers Hagar to Abram, presumably so that she will retain some status, and the child will be considered hers in some legal capacity. To do so, she must promote her maid, at least according to 16:3, to the status of wife. While Hagar may not have had any say in the matter, Sarai is not only creating a means for Hagar to have a child, something from Sarai's perspective that is clearly positive, but is also prepared to promote her to do so. While commentators have made comparisons between what Sarai is forcing upon Hagar and what happens to Sarai in Egypt, there is no discussion in the text that Sarai had any status in the house of Pharaoh; on the other hand, here Hagar seems to be promoted, a considerable promotion. The "promotion" offered Hagar is not far from that granted to Zilpah and Bilhah, the maids belonging to Leah and Rachel respectively (29:24, 29). Both bear children "upon the knees" of the mistresses, sons that are counted as those of the "wives" (30:3–13). And yet the maids' children, because of the maids' unique relationships with their mistresses, inherit with the mistresses' sons. As a result, the biological mothers are somewhat protected.[21] In those cases, there is little discussion in the literature about the severe actions taken to fulfill the whims of the master.

Trouble occurs after Hagar conceives. According to 16:4 Abram cohabits with Hagar, she conceives, and when she sees that she has conceived, she perpetrates some action toward her mistress. This verse is in the voice of the narrator, who is recounting what happens. It therefore is not Sarai's opinion of the situation, but what the narrator states actually is the situation.[22] The problem is how to translate the verb and how severe the action is. The verb at issue is from the root *qof-lamed-lamed* (*qalal*). According to NJPS her mistress "was lowered in her esteem," which is a personal affront but nothing outrageously momentous. The RSV treats the problem as a bit worse: "She looked with contempt on her mistress." The KJV goes so far as to say, "Her mistress was despised in her eyes." The problem concerns the meaning of the root. According to Brown, Driver, and Briggs, the term has a base meaning of "be slight," and in transitive use (as here) means to "despise," count as "trifling."[23]

A better way to understand the meaning is to examine other verses where the term appears and see how it is treated. According to Exod 21:17, one who insults (*qalal*) a parent should be killed. In 1 Kgs 2:8, despite the fact that someone did this (*qalal*) to David, David swears not to put him to the sword. In Gen 12:3 whoever takes this very (*qalal*) action against Abram will draw a serious curse from the Deity. According to the biblical text, the (*qalal*) action is severe. In the Deity's opinion, such a human action is so severe that if someone does it to Abram, the Deity would curse that individual in an even more serious way (*'arar*, 12:3; see ch. 2, above).

In the next verse (16:5) Sarai raises the issue with Abram and implies that the wrong done to her is his fault. She says she gave her slave into his bosom, and now that she is pregnant, Sarai is the target of contempt (*qalal*). She appeals to the Deity to judge between her and Abram. Sarai does not reprimand Hagar herself but goes to Abram, von Rad claims, because of the legal situation, according to which Hagar now belongs to Abram.[24] In fact, von Rad goes so far as to claim that Sarai's comment, "The wrong to me is upon you" (16:5), really means, "The wrong that has happened to me is your responsibility," because he is the one who could restore her rights.[25]

Sarai also brings the Deity into the argument. Up to this point in the narrative, there has been no direct contact between the Deity and Sarai. While the Deity saves Sarai in the Egyptian episode, the text gives no indication that Sarai knows this. Sarai is not privy to Abram's conversations with the Deity, and yet she is the one who is prepared to have the Deity decide on their actions. Rather than going to the Deity, Abram abdicates all responsibility and tells Sarai that her maid is in her hand, to do what is right in her own eyes.

Von Rad takes this to mean that although earlier Sarai gives Hagar to Abram, now he is giving Hagar back to Sarai.[26] He goes on to say that the "abuse" Hagar suffers at Sarai's hand is the loss of her newly gained status.[27] While Hagar may have lost her status, the nature of the abuse is clearly more severe than that. One of the problems is that often in the biblical text, when someone does what is right in their own eyes, it is not good. At this point Sarai "humbles" Hagar. The term is from the root *ayin-nun-he* (*'anah*) which has a base meaning of "be bowed down, afflicted," and thus in transitive use means to "afflict."[28] There are a number of cases where the term is used. An ironic twist is that this is the root used for what the Egyptians later do to the Israelites (Exod 1:11–12). In a further ironic note, according to Exod 1:12, the more the Egyptians "oppressed" (*'anah*) the Israelites, the more they increased and spread. Here again, the verb is used for oppression with resulting fertility, but with the oppressors' peoplehood reversed.

Sarai is not upset that Hagar is pregnant; her anger stems from Hagar's reaction to Sarai as a result of her pregnancy. The literature often takes Sarai to task for her high level of rage, especially from a woman whom the text has discussed periodically for four chapters and here for the first time lets the reader hear her voice.

In discussing the conflict between Sarai and Hagar, commentators often research ancient Near Eastern law and relationships between master/mistress and slave, especially when there are women and children involved. The ancient Near Eastern material is important because ruling bodies legislated many of these issues at various places in different periods. Though there are problems with understanding the role that ancient law codes played in their own context and how that would impact the biblical text, we can use them to reveal issues faced by ancient peoples.[29] We should not see them as hard and fast laws applied everywhere in the ancient Near East in all periods, but rather as ways, idealized or practical, that ancient people used to adjudicate difficult societal issues. However, there are no extant "law codes" from the region of Syro-Palestine dated anywhere near what could be considered the time of the patriarchs. Thus, it is impossible for us to know what rules functioned or were formulated at the time when any of these characters might have existed or been created.

Despite the problems with the ancient Near Eastern law codes, readers must still examine them since they reflect a number of different topics within the Sarai-Hagar story, though none of them explicitly deal with exactly this type of episode. One issue concerns giving a slave to bear children for someone. The ancient law codes reflect the situation that not all women could bear children, men married more than one woman, and slaves bore children for their mistresses.[30] The Code of Hammurabi is useful in this regard. This appears to be a collection of rules compiled toward the end of the forty-two-year reign of Hammurabi (ca 1792–1750 B.C.E.), who was the sixth ruler of the First Dynasty of Babylon.[31] This king is one of the more famous from the history of the ancient Near East because he directed a great political expansion of his empire and organized a complex and sophisticated government and military bureaucracy to administer it.[32] His collection of rules is the longest and best organized law collection from Mesopotamia, including between 275 and 300 law provisions.[33] Despite the large range of topics addressed in his laws, there is only one law that addresses the specific issue of a woman giving her husband a slave specifically, and this is number 146 in his code:

> If a man marries a *nadītu* and she gives a slave woman to her
> husband and she (the slave) then bears children, after which that
> slave woman aspires to equal status with her mistress—because she
> bore children, her mistress will not sell her; she shall place upon her
> the slave-lock, and she shall reckon her with the slave women.[34]

What this law addresses is the situation where a woman who is not
allowed (see below) to bear children provides a slave to do so. Such a law
existing in the Code of Hammurabi shows that a slave becoming pregnant on the wife's behalf for the master's child did not first occur in
Genesis. Since the Babylonians legislate such a topic, this must mean that
the issue was, if not common, regular enough to need adjudication. The
nature of the pronouncement means that in some concept of law in
Hammurabi's Babylon, in this situation, the person at fault is the slave.

The problem with this reference is that it addresses the specific context of a *nadītu* woman. A *nadītu* woman was a type of ancient nun, who
could be married but was not allowed to bear children.[35] Like many other
offices in Mesopotamia, the status of the *nadītu* women, who they were,
what their responsibilities were, what they could not do—these varied
among the different periods in Mesopotamian history. It therefore is difficult to determine precisely what understanding of a *nadītu* might be relevant to Sarai.[36] Finally, there is no evidence in the text that Sarai is a
nadītu woman of any sort.

The rule of the Code of Hammurabi number 147 takes the issue a bit
further and leads to the next topic: "If she does not bear children, her mistress shall sell her." Thus, if the slave woman bears children, she is protected but kept as a slave. If she does not bear, her punishment is to be
sold. In both cases the woman who is "mistress" and her status are protected, and a slave, fertile or not, should not forget their status. Again, this
case is different in that *nadītu* women were not necessarily barren but
they were not usually allowed to bear children.

To explore this issue we also need to address the roles of slavery and
the relationship between master and slave. The subject of slavery is complicated in the United States, where plantation slavery was the norm and
the definition of slavery was a racial matter. Such was not the case in the
ancient Near East: in most cases, a family owned a few slaves, and one
became a slave through war or financial distress.[37] In the ancient Near
East there were several forms of slavery. To a large extent—at least in the
Mesopotamian worldview, by which people were formed so that the gods

did not have to work—everyone was a slave to someone.[38] As a result, it was important to legislate the relationships between the different classes of people to maintain order.[39] As early as 2100 B.C.E., the Laws of Ur Nammu number 25 state: "If a slave woman curses someone acting with the authority of her mistress, they shall scour her mouth with one sila of salt."[40] Even the biblical text has a reference to the importance of slaves obeying their masters, in Prov 30:21–23:

> The earth shudders at three things, at four which it cannot bear:
> A slave who becomes king; A scoundrel sated with food; A loath-
> some woman who gets married; A slave-girl who supplants her
> mistress. (NJPS)

What this means, according to the text, is that while Sarai's actions may not seem "nice," especially to a modern Western audience, they are consistent with ancient Near Eastern and biblical tradition. Sarai has not borne children to her husband, an important man in the region, and she makes a suggestion to resolve the situation. Her resolution is in keeping with ancient Near Eastern tradition and is not out of line with anything the Deity thus far has commanded or even suggested to Abram. Sarai may even have promoted Hagar in the process. Following conception, Hagar's attitude changes, first reported by the narrator of the text, and then also in Sarai's complaint to her husband. Sarai's actions, while admittedly harsh even according to the text, are also not out of line with the text's later suggestions about dealing with slaves (Prov 30:21–23), Abram's treatment of Hagar (whom he apparently demotes by transferring her back into Sarai's hand), or the Deity, who is about to bless Hagar.

Hagar's Retreat to the Desert: Genesis 16:7–16

Hagar is not the focus of this study, but some of her actions must be considered since they heavily impact perceptions of Sarai. Hagar's interactions with the Deity, or the Deity's messenger, and the role of her son are major components of what impacts Sarai and her relations with the other major characters in the story. Again, as was the case with Gen 13–14, though Sarai does not necessarily appear in this textual block, the activities of the surrounding characters change who they are and their relationship with the Deity. As a result, Sarai is changed. It is also significant that Hagar is the only woman in the Hebrew Bible reported to dialogue with the Deity in earthly manifestation, at least the Deity's messenger. The Deity's treatment of Hagar and the promises to, and demands of, her signify the Deity's understanding of the role and importance of her character.

Hagar's response to Sarai's treatment is to flee, verifying for many the harshness of her actions. In recent years Hagar has received new attention, especially in feminist and womanist literature.[41] One of the issues magnifying her role as the downtrodden slave is the way she is treated in the New Testament (Gal 4:21–31). Since the goal of this study is to understand the role of Sarai and her contemporaries in the Hebrew Bible, the New Testament reference merely confuses the issue. It is but one ancient interpretation of the text, and it carries an ideological motivation. Yet this interpretation certainly has colored many perceptions of who Hagar is and how she should be treated; but it will not be considered at this point.[42]

The text states categorically that Hagar runs away, clearly of her own volition (Gen 16:6). For some modern interpreters, this is Hagar taking charge of her life.[43] According to ancient Near Eastern law, a slave running away is a serious crime, as is providing refuge to a runaway slave.[44] Since the messenger of the Deity will later tell her to return to her mistress, it appears that the biblical text is cognizant of ancient Near Eastern customs concerning the role of slaves.

When the messenger of the Deity (often translated as "angel") finds her, she is by a spring of water in the wilderness or desert, on the way to Shur.[45] Rulon-Miller observes that the wilderness of Shur seems a hospitable place for Hagar since it is near her native Egypt.[46] While the text never explains how Hagar becomes a slave, there is no evidence in the text that when she is in Egypt she is free, or that Sarai and Abram originally enslave her. In the biblical text the concept of slavery is complex. Although the Israelite experience of slavery is problematic, even the Hebrew Bible condemns not the institution of slavery but rather the way it is managed, particularly in Egypt. Furthermore, one element of the Egyptian references is that Hagar is not like Abram and Sarai: she is different and foreign. When Hagar is about to bear the first child to the first patriarch of Israel, her possible return to Egypt—which may or may not provide an easier life for her—certainly makes a comment about the risks of trusting foreign women. This is a theme that reappears throughout the Hebrew Bible.

The Deity's messenger begins the conversation by calling her "Hagar" (Gen 16:8)—the only character in the story who does this.[47] At the same time she is qualified as "maid of Sarai" (16:8). Regardless of any status change Hagar may have experienced earlier (16:3), she has either reverted back to her slave status or remained so in the consideration of the Deity. The messenger asks from where Hagar came and to where she is going (16:8). Hagar responds, though not directly to the questions asked, by admitting that she is running away from her "mistress Sarai" (16:8). This verse indicates that Hagar, like the messenger, considers herself still in some sort of slave status to Sarai.

The messenger follows Hagar's comment by telling her to go back and submit to her harsh treatment (16:9), at least recognizing her plight though sending her back to it. The messenger's command (using the imperative) is then qualified by a blessing granted her: "I [apparently referring now directly to the Deity rather than the messenger] will greatly increase your [Hagar's] offspring, and they shall be too many to count" (16:10). This blessing is similar to the one granted Abram in the previous chapter (15:5), though without the land offer. The messenger promises that Hagar will have a son and describes him a bit (16:11–12). Hagar names the Deity who speaks to her, and that name identifies the well where the conversation occurs (16:14).[48] The final action of the chapter is that Hagar bears a son to Abram, who names him Ishmael.

Hagar's story is significant in our context for a number of reasons. Genesis 16 ends with the fulfillment of Sarai's original plan in 16:2: Abram has a child through Sarai's maid Hagar. The Deity, while prepared to let Hagar suffer through Sarai's harsh treatment, is also prepared to offer her what other women do not usually receive, a blessing directly from the Deity and an increase of her offspring (and in 16:10 this is identified as *her* offspring, not specified as Abram's).

On the one hand the Deity's reaction to Hagar could be considered hypocritical. The Deity offers her things few women receive and yet at the same time is prepared to keep her a slave. In fact, Trible accuses the Deity of identifying "here not with the suffering slave but with her oppressors."[49] The Deity's actions may not be so hypocritical and callous as it first appears. If slavery is considered a condition that, while not positive, is part of the world order, than the Deity is not prepared at the time to change that world order. Later legislation in Leviticus ameliorates some conditions of slavery but does not abolish it. Slavery is especially problematic when it is the systematic enslavement of an entire people, as reported in the book of Exodus, an event foreshadowed by an ancestor of the Israelites having an Egyptian slave.

Sarai's Role in the Promise: Genesis 17

To some extent chapter 17 legitimates Sarai's actions concerning Hagar and the blessing of Hagar's descendents. In Gen 17 Sarai and Abram's names are changed, and Sarah is named as the correct mother of the heir to the Deity's promises. The connections between Gen 16 and 17 are seldom noted because the chapters are not treated together. The Masoretes, while recognizing a break at the end of Gen 16, definitely see a significant break at the end of Gen 17. In fact, the end of Gen 17 is the end of the parashah (weekly reading) that begins with Gen 12:1. Thus, according to their interpretation, the stories of Abram's wanderings begin with this command by the Deity in 12:1 and end with the circumcision of his household, which occurs at the end of Gen 17. As a result, Gen 16 and 17 are more closely connected than Gen 17 and 18, despite the fact that, to some extent, much of Gen 18 is a repetition, in the hearing of Sarah, of what the Deity tells Abram in Gen 17.

Genesis 17 begins with referring to Abram's age. According to the previous chapter, Abram is eighty-six years old when Hagar bears Ishmael to him (16:16). One verse later Abram is ninety-nine years old (17:1). The next verse is another statement that the Deity promises to establish the Deity's covenant with Abram (17:2). The Deity repeats the terms of the covenant: Abram will be the father of a multitude of nations (Gen 17:4). Then the Deity changes Abram's name, stating that he will no longer be called Abram, but his name shall be Abraham because the Deity is making him the father of a multitude of nations (17:5). The Deity promises to maintain the covenant with Abram and his offspring to come (17:7). Also, the Deity will assign the land in which Abraham is sojourning to him and his offspring as an everlasting covenant (17:8). On some levels the name change could be considered the Deity fulfilling the promise of 12:2. There the Deity states literally that the Deity will make Abram's name "big." Here, by adding another consonant to his name, the Deity actually carries through with the promise, literally, though few, the present author included, believe a simple name change to be the major thrust of the Deity's promise in 12:2.

The Deity then moves on to the harder part of the covenant. Abraham and his descendants shall keep the covenant, and the practice of circumcision is their side of the bargain (17:10). The Deity details the signs of the covenant and clarifies that this shall be a tradition throughout the generations: all males born in his household shall be circumcised at eight days of age (17:12).

The details of circumcision and the references to Abraham living a long life and dying peacefully are new, but the rest of the covenant described here has already been mentioned in one form or another by the Deity (12:2; 12:7; 13:15–16; 15:15). Abraham does not complain to the Deity about a lack of offspring, as he does in Gen 15, and everything the Deity says in Gen 17 thus far could be in keeping with understanding Ishmael as the intended heir. The references to Abraham's age at the end of Gen 16 and again in the first line Gen 17 indicate that Ishmael is thirteen years old. All signs promote the idea that, in the eyes of both the Deity and Abraham, Ishmael is the intended heir. One can even understand the promises in Gen 17:4–14 as reconfirming Ishmael's status since nothing new is really offered Abraham (other than a new name), and the Deity places a responsibility on him and his family.

The Masoretes insert a small break after 17:14, understanding the conversation with Abraham about circumcision as different from the one concerning Sarai's name change and the announcement of the birth of Isaac. Turner also identifies a shift here, claiming that before 17:15 everything in Gen 17 indicates that Ishmael is the birthright son.[50] Even the introduction of Sarai in 17:15 does not change the notion that Ishmael is still the legitimate heir; 17:15 focuses on Sarai, and only in 17:16 does the Deity name her as the mother of the heir to the promise.

The way the Deity changes Sarai's name is different from Abraham's name change. Her name change occurs before her shift in status, making her the mother of the heir to the promise. This name change again indicates that there is something about Sarai herself that is important, not just the fact that Abraham is her spouse. When changing Abram's name, the Deity states, "And one will no longer call your name Abram because your name will be Abraham" (17:5). The Deity even provides a reason why the Deity is changing his name: Abraham will become the father of many nations. The formulation for Sarai's name change is quite different. The Deity speaks directly to Abraham by using the second person singular: "Sarai, your wife, you will no longer call her name Sarai because Sarah is her name" (17:15). The phrasing is directed to Abraham, and the text offers no reason for the change. There is also little difference in the meaning of the name.[51] The way the sentence is phrased is almost as though the Deity is not changing her name but correcting Abraham, as though he was calling her the wrong name all along. As opposed to Abraham's case, the text does not state that something new is happening but states definitively, "Sarah is her name" (17:15). While the difference in translation may seem minor, Abraham's mistake over her name may also be why he never before understood her importance, which the Deity sees and is about to make explicit.

In the next verse the Deity continues by promising to bless Sarah and give Abraham a son by her (17:16). In the same verse, the Deity claims to bless Sarah, but in this case the blessing is so that she will give rise to nations, and rulers of peoples will issue from her. In this case, the Deity is quite explicit that Sarah receives a new or corrected name, which in either case puts her in the same category as Abraham, who recently received a new name. The Deity *twice* states categorically that he will bless her and that she will have a son (17:16, 19). There is nothing subtle about the Deity's intentions or stance on the matter. The text has just introduced the novel concept that Sarah's maternity will be as important as Abraham's paternity.[52]

Abraham's response is one that many have had to explain away because it reveals so little respect for the Deity and Sarah. Abraham literally "fell upon his face and laughed" (17:17). His laughter is not hidden, but the reason for his laughter is verbalized only in his heart, a distinction that will become important later. According to Abraham, the reason for his laughter is that he wonders whether a child can be born to a man one hundred years old, or to Sarah at age ninety. He is laughing at precisely what the Deity has just told him is going to happen.

Despite the clear focus of Abraham's laughter, commentators find legitimate reasons for Abraham's behavior rather than attributing it to disbelief in the Deity. Speiser translates Abraham's action as "smiled" rather than "laughed," observing that it is a wordplay on the name Isaac, though "laugh" would work just as well.[53] Later, when Sarah carries out the identical action (though using the feminine form), Speiser renders the same verb as "laughed," with no comment about wordplay.[54] Von Rad translates the verb as "laughed" in both places but claims that Abraham's laughter has a logical explanation: "Abraham's laugh brings us in any case to the outer limits of what is psychologically possible. Combined with the pathetic gesture of reverence is an almost horrible laugh, deadly earnest, not in fun, bringing belief and unbelief close together."[55] Von Rad then sees Sarah's later laughter as "standing out from the mutely attentive Abraham," and he lists a number of references where a woman is used as a negative figure of contrast.[56] The issue motivating translation technique and interpretative methodology appears to be that Abraham is the faithful one who is attentive to the Deity, and the text must be translated and interpreted to uphold that thesis, whether the text supports the interpretation or not. In fact, Speiser almost admits as much when he claims,

"The concept of Abraham in a derisive attitude toward God would be decidedly out of keeping with P's character. The above translation [smiled instead of laughed], therefore, should come close to the spirit of the received text, though not the original use of the pertinent verb."[57]

Regardless of commentators' distress with what the text actually states, the next verse reinforces Abraham's discomfort with the situation: "O that Ishmael might live by your favor" (17:18), he implores. This is not a proclamation of joy or excitement at the pending news. Abraham, not the Deity, raises the possibility of Ishmael as the heir. The Deity has just promised a son by Sarah and even changed her name, thereby placing her in a status similar to Abraham (17:15–16). Again the Deity, without touching the question of Ishmael as Abraham's heir, assures Abraham that a son would be born to him through Sarah. Abraham's statement clearly indicates that Abraham considers Ishmael his descendent and heir to the promise.[58] Yet the Deity has not yet stated that the new son, born of Sarah, would dislodge Ishmael from the position he presently holds. As Turner declares, "Abraham *has* one son who will be greatly blessed, and he *will* have another son with whom Yahweh 'will establish his covenant' (whatever that means)."[59] Thus, Abraham's lack of enthusiasm at the concept of another descendent is even more shocking.

The Deity, as all along, has nothing against Ishmael, and even from the announcement of his birth has intended a role for him (16:11–12). Neither the Deity nor the narrator has thus far shown any sign that the birth of another son for Abraham is going to change that. Yet the Deity is adamant, as is revealed in the next verse, that Sarah, "your [Abraham's] wife," will bear a son, whom he shall name "Isaac" (17:19). Only at this point, after Abraham makes a case for Ishmael, does the Deity state categorically that the Deity will maintain the covenant with Isaac as an everlasting covenant for his offspring to come (17:19). Before Abraham can say another word, the Deity continues that the Deity has heeded Abraham concerning Ishmael and will bless him and make him fertile and numerous; he shall be the father of twelve chieftains, and the Deity will make Ishmael a great nation (17:20; fulfilled, 25:12–18). Before finishing the conversation the Deity reinforces that the covenant will be with Isaac, whom Sarah shall bear to Abraham the next year (17:21). Before Abraham can say another word, the text reports that the Deity finishes speaking with Abraham, and the Deity was gone from him (17:22).

The rest of the chapter concerns the circumcision of Abraham's household. The verse immediately following Abraham's conversation with the Deity has Abraham taking all the males in his household and circumcising them on the very day that the Deity spoke to him (17:23). The first one named on the list is Ishmael, identified by the narrator as his son (17:23). Thus, Abraham immediately fulfills the obligation of circumcision that the Deity commands of him; yet his first action shows his commitment to the son he already has. Turner observes that Abraham's final act in Gen 17 does not dismiss Ishmael from consideration but binds him closer to Abraham, and possibly to the Deity.[60]

We may not consider circumcising Ishmael, the only existing son, as a major infraction at this point in the story. However, the following chapter shows that Abraham makes little or no attempt to communicate with anyone, including Sarah, about the Deity's announcement that she will have a son who will be the heir to the covenant with the Deity. Abraham's actions immediately following his conversation with the Deity in Gen 17 reveal his commitment to the Deity but also to Ishmael. By not announcing that a new son is to be born, and by naming Ishmael as his son and first in the practice that physically reveals a commitment to the covenant—Abraham thereby lifts up his relationship with Ishmael in the eyes of his household and Sarah.

Sarah does not appear or carry out any actions in Gen 17, and yet her life is changed by the conversation between the Deity and Abraham. The Deity emphasizes the importance of Sarah in the covenant and the future of Abraham's descendants by changing her name and then establishing her, in no uncertain terms, as the mother of the future heir. Abraham's response is first laughter and then a request for Ishmael's recognition as the heir. The Deity takes note of Ishmael but once again is the one who must defend Sarah and remind Abraham of her importance. Despite the Deity's clarity as to who will be the heir of the promise, Abraham makes no move to reveal that or show his agreement to that cause. All of these factors are background for some of Sarah's later actions, and we must analyze her behavior in light of Abraham's treatment of her throughout Genesis.

Conclusions

The Masoretes interpret the separation between Gen 17 and 18 as a major break, ending the parashah that begins with Gen 12:1. There is a neat symmetry to the parashah: it begins with Abram's journey to a new land, separating from the old, and ending with circumcision, a rite practiced in Canaan but not in Mesopotamia.[61] Since Abraham also circumcises his entire household, it is on some level a fulfillment of the relationship between Abraham and the Deity, with the broad parameters of the covenant defined. On the one hand the parashah ends with a note of obedience (circumcision); yet it also ends on a note of expectation. The initial promise is that the Deity will provide offspring. In this final segment Abraham has both offspring (Ishmael) and the promise of more offspring. The next chapter, where the Deity again announces future offspring for Abraham and Sarah, ties neatly to Gen 17 and yet involves different players in various roles.

Most of the members in Abraham's family's status have changed radically in these chapters (Gen 14–17). In the beginning of Gen 14 Abram becomes an important player in regional and international politics, while Lot is a victim whom his uncle must save. The events even seem to change, or certainly modify, Abram's relationship with his Deity. The shift in who and what Abram is in the region appears to impact Sarai, who initiates actions that might bring the Deity's promise of progeny to fruition. For reasons not predicted by Sarai, her plans do not follow her intended path. Hagar becomes a player in the family dynamics and an important character. She has her own conversation with the Deity, and in due time bears a son to Abram.

Rather than accomplishing a promotion in the family, Sarai's plans seem to backfire. In Gen 17 the Deity moves into the situation to clarify finally what Sarah's status will be in the family. The Deity introduces the promise that Abraham will have *another* son, and that son will be the one to inherit the promise. Abraham's reaction to the news is lukewarm at best. The Deity's final request is the circumcision of every male in Abraham's household, which he carries out immediately, especially on his son, Ishmael, thereby bringing him into the covenant.

The roles of many of the major players are introduced and established in the parashah of these opening chapters, with little resolution. Abraham's position with the Deity is secure, but the generational transition is not clear. Lot, so prominent earlier in the narrative, has receded, though he is not yet completely out of the picture. The Deity promises Hagar that her son's offspring will become an exceedingly great multitude, but the context is not clear. Only near the end of the parashah (17:15–21) does the Deity promise Sarah a role in the future covenant. However, no one yet conveys that information to Sarah, and the path to achieve that promise is not going to be smooth.

Notes

1. W. Brueggemann, *Genesis* (Interpretation; Atlanta: John Knox, 1982), 134.
2. For example: E. A. Speiser, *Genesis* (Anchor Bible; Garden City, N.Y.: Doubleday, 1985), 105–9; and G. von Rad, *Genesis: A Commentary* (Old Testament Library; Philadelphia: Westminster, 1972), 175.
3. Shinar is a name for the region of Babylonia. J. A. Davila, "Shinar," *ABD* 5:1220.
4. The location of Ellasar was unclear already to ancient interpreters who either do not translate it or place it variously in Larsa, capital of one of the two principal cities in southern Mesopotamia in the Isin-Larsa period; in Assur, the capital of Assyria for much of her history; or even in Armenia. M. Astour, "Ellasar," *ABD* 2:476–77.
5. This is ancient Susiana or modern Iran. F. Vallat, "Elam," 2:424.
6. Since the term *goyim* means "nations" in Hebrew, many ancient versions simply translate the Hebrew word. Other possibilities are Guti, a people in the Zagros Mountains; a Hittite king named Tudhaliyas; or even the Assyrian king Sennacherib. M. C. Astour, "Goiim," *ABD* 2:1057.
7. BDB, 335, *khanikh*, understanding the term as an adjective meaning "trained, tried, experienced." These men thus are tried and trusty.
8. Though the name does not occur elsewhere in the Hebrew Bible, it is mentioned in Jdt 4:4; 15:5; and perhaps 15:4. H. O. Thompson, "Hobah," *ABD* 3:235.
9. The text states "1/10 of all," but does not specify "of what": all he has with him, all he has? The text does not clarify.
10. For example, von Rad's translation does not place Abram's name in brackets to indicate that it is inserted but proceeds as though the change of subject to Abram were in the text. Von Rad, *Genesis*, 174.
11. Tempted by the same attitude are several judges in the book of Judges who claim responsibility for victories they should have credited to the Israelite Deity, or who fight for the wrong reasons. Examples are Barak (Judg 4–5), Jerubbaal/Gideon (6:9), Jephthah (11), and Samson (13–16). For a discussion on how they should have credited the Deity with their victories, see T. Schneider, *Judges* (Berit Olam; Collegeville: Liturgical Press, 2000).
12. In the Hebrew Bible the river/brook of Egypt is used both as a geographical reference to the southern border of Judah (Num 34:5; Josh 15:4, 47; 1 Kgs 8:65; 2 Chr 7:8; Ezek 47:19, 48:28) and as an element in the phrase "from the brook/river of Egypt to the river Euphrates," which designates the portion of Syro-Palestine between the northeast and southern borders claimed by Israel and Judah. The term is also used by the Assyrians in documents from the Assyrian kings. Tiglath-pilesar III (745–727 B.C.E.), Sargon II (721–705 B.C.E.), and Esarhaddon (680-664 B.C.E.). Even with all these references, locating the brook/river of Egypt is difficult. Scholars associate the brook/river of Egypt either with the Nahal Besor or Wadi el 'Arish. See M. Görg, "Egypt, Brook of" *ABD* 2:321.
13. In Gen 11:20 the text already states that she is barren and has no child. In 16:1 the text does not state that she is barren but that she has borne no children to

Abram, thus changing the state of Sarai. She is not necessarily barren but has the potential to bear and has happened not to bear any children to Abram. This leaves open the possibility that she has actually borne a child to someone else, especially noteworthy in view of the episode in Egypt and her time with Pharaoh.

14. BDB, 1046, translates "maid, maid-servant."

15. BDB, 125.

16. Brueggemann, *Genesis*, 151.

17. P. Trible, *Texts of Terror: Literary-Feminist Readings of Biblical Narratives* (Overtures to Biblical Theology; Philadelphia: Fortress, 1984), 9.

18. J. C. Exum, "Who's Afraid of 'The Endangered Ancestress'?" in *Women in the Hebrew Bible: A Reader* (ed. A. Bach; New York: Routledge, 1999), 142.

19. N. Steinberg, *Kinship and Marriage in Genesis: A Household Economics Perspective* (Minneapolis: Fortress, 1993), 61.

20. Speiser bases his translation on the Akkadian cognate *assatum* that may signify either "wife" or "concubine." Speiser, *Genesis*, 116–17. All the reference in *CAD* for *assatum* translate as "wife." *CAD*, vol. 1: *A, Part 2*, 463–65.

21. Following the birth of their children, the status of Bilhah and Zilpah is not precisely clear. Yet when they leave Haran with Jacob's entourage and Laban pursues them in search of the household *teraphim*, the maids have their own tent, described in the same way as Rachel and Leah's tents (31:33). For a more detailed discussion on the banishment of Ishmael (21:10), see chapter 5, below.

22. S. Pace Jeansonne, *The Women of Genesis: From Sarah to Potiphar's Wife* (Minneapolis: Fortress, 1990), 20.

23. BDB, 886.

24. Von Rad, *Genesis*, 192.

25. Ibid.

26. Ibid., 192–93

27. Ibid.

28. BDB, 776: the form here is the Piel of *'anah*, thus meaning "humble, mishandle, afflict."

29. For a good discussion of the problems surrounding the role and function of the Code of Hammurabi, one of the most famous ancient collections of regulations, see Jean Bottero, "The Code of Hammurabi," in *Mesopotamia: Writing, Reasoning and the Gods* (Chicago: University of Chicago Press, 1992), 156–84. For an introduction to general law, see Samuel Greengus, "Legal and Social Institutions of Ancient Mesopotamia," in *Civilizations of the Ancient Near East* (ed. Jack Sasson; New York: Charles Scribner's Sons, 1995), 469–84.

30. The law collections were all fairly recently published in a convenient and thorough source: M. Roth, *Law Collections from Mesopotamia and Asia Minor* (SBL Writings from the Ancient World; Atlanta: Scholars Press, 1995). The volume also includes a fine summary about the source and context of each of codes under discussion.

31. Ibid., 71.

32. Ibid.

33. Ibid.

34. Ibid., 109.

35. The role and status of the *nadītu* women in Mesopotamia changed over time and place. The *nadītu* women of Sippar in the Old Babylonian period (1950-1595 B.C.E.) were cloistered—could not marry—but could have children who were adopted by the *nadītu's* brother upon birth. From the laws in the Code of Hammurabi and other references, it is clear that *nadītu* women in Old Babylonian Babylon could marry but not have children. The references do not address if the women were married but could not engage in intercourse, or if they used some sort of birth control. See "Naditu A," in *CAD*, vol. 11: *N, Part 1,* 63 and Norman Yoffee, "The Economy of Ancient Western Asia," *Civilizations of the Ancient Near East,* vol. 3 (ed. J. M. Sasson; New York: Charles Scribner's Sons, 1995), 1395–96.

36. N. Yoffee, "The Economy of Ancient Western Asia," 195–96.

37. M. A. Dandamayev, "Slavery (ANE)," *ABD* 6:58–62.

38. I. M. Diakonoff, "Slave-Labour vs. Non-Slave Labour: The Problem of Definition," in *Labor in the Ancient Near East* (ed. M. A. Powell; Copenhagen: Akademisk Forlag, 1987).

39. The Code of Hammurabi deals with three major classes of people—*awīlum, mushkēnum,* and *wardum*—and many laws specify different penalties depending on the class of the victim and the class of the perpetrator.

40. Roth, *Law Collections,* 20.

41. Among others, see Trible, *Texts of Terror,* 9–36; Nina Rulon-Miller, "Hagar: A Woman with an Attitude," in *The World of Genesis: Persons, Places, Perspectives* (ed. P. R. Davies and D. J. A. Clines; JSOTSup 257; Sheffield: Sheffield Academic Press, 1998), 60–89; S. Teubal, *Hagar the Egyptian: The Lost Tradition of the Matriarchs* (San Francisco: Harper & Row, 1990).

42. The "Conclusions" chapter and the Appendix will briefly consider the role of the New Testament in interpreting the texts concerning Sarah, Abraham, and Hagar.

43. Trible, *Texts of Terror,* 13.

44. Ancient Near Eastern law codes address the role of the runaway slave and legislate what is to happen to the slave (Laws of Eshnunna 51–52, probably Laws of Hammurabi only partially preserved because they are in the gap of lines ii.14–iii.34), a person finding and harboring a slave (Laws of Lipit-Ishtar 12–14; Laws of Eshnunna 49; Laws of Hammurabi 7, 16), and a person returning a runaway slave (Laws of Ur Nammu 17; Laws of Hammurabi 17–20). In all cases a slave must be returned; someone who does not return a slave is also at fault. For all of these, see Roth, *Law Collections.*

45. According to D. Seely, "Shur," *ABD* 5:1230, it is perhaps a place located in the northern Sinai between the border of Canaan and the border of Egypt. Ironically, according to Exod 15:22–26, the area is between the Red Sea and Marah and is where Israel murmured for water. In the later patriarchal narratives, Abraham will later dwell between Kadesh and Shur before moving to Gerar (Gen 20:1). The descendants of Ishmael also lived in the area from Havilah to Shur (25:18).

46. Rulon-Miller, "Hagar," 76.

47. Ibid.

48. In another ironic twist, Isaac is settled in the Negev and has left (or come to) this same Beer-lahai-roi when Abraham's servant returns with Rebekah (Gen 24: 62). For more discussion of this, see chapter 6, "Sarah's End" (below).

49. Trible, *Texts of Terror*, 22, claims that the Deity identifies not with the suffering slave but with her oppressors.

50. L. A. Turner, *Announcement of Plot in Genesis* (JSOTSup 96; Sheffield: JSOT Press, 1990), 77.

51. According to Speiser, *Genesis*, 125, Sarah embodies the common feminine ending, and Sarai preserves an old and specialized feminine form.

52. Turrner, *Announcement of Plot*, 77

53. Speiser, *Genesis*, 123.

54. Ibid.

55. Ibid., 203.

56. Von Rad, *Genesis*, 208.

57. Speiser, *Genesis*, 128.

58. Turner, *Announcement of Plot*, 77.

59. Ibid.

60. Ibid., 78.

61. R. H. Hall, "Circumcision," *ABD* 1:1025.

CHAPTER 4

The Three Messengers' Announcement: Genesis 18–19

Genesis 18 includes accounts of the Deity's messengers' visit to Abraham and Abraham's discussion with the Deity about how many righteous individuals need to live in Sodom and Gomorrah in order to save the cities. The episode is followed by the destruction of Sodom and Gomorrah (Gen 19). Scholars waver as to where the breaks in these episodes occur, though most separate the conversation between the messengers and Sarah and Abraham from the discussion between Abraham and the Deity.[1] Most then connect the second half of Gen 18 with Gen 19.[2]

On one level there does seem to be a shift from the text's subject in 18:1–15 to the discussion about Sodom and Gomorrah in 18:16–33, and Gen 19 continues to focus on those cities. Treating Gen 18–19 as one unit, or treating 18:1–15 as a separate unit—either way makes the issue of the impending destruction of Sodom and Gomorrah the central focus of the two chapters. Genesis 18:1–15 is related through the appearance of the messengers, and therefore the matters raised in 18:1–15 are subsumed under the greater issue of the judgment on Sodom and Gomorrah.

The Masoretes include no break in Gen 18. My original intention was to go against the Masoretic tradition and treat the two separately because

my translation of parts of 18:1–15 are somewhat different from traditional translations. Treating the unit separately would highlight the differences
in my translation. It soon became clear, however, that when we study the
episodes together, we can more clearly see a number of issues running
through both incidents, which modern interpretations tend to separate.
The issues highlighted by treating Gen 18 as one unit are particularly relevant for understanding Sarah and Abraham's relationship to each other
and to the Deity. Hence, following the Masoretic tradition, I will treat this
chapter as one unit. Furthermore, once Gen 18 is treated as its own unit
with a cohesive topic running through it, the role of Sodom and Gomorrah's demise becomes less important and other issues in chapter 18, often
neglected when 18:1–15 are separated, become more obvious.

Who, What, Where, and When: Genesis 18:1–5

The chapter begins following what, for the Masoretes, is a sizeable break
in the text. The last chapter (17) includes some particularly noteworthy
announcements and actions: the Deity changes Abram's name to Abraham, blesses him, changes Sarai's name to Sarah, blesses her, and announces to Abraham that Sarah will bear a son to be heir to the promise;
finally, Abraham circumcises the males of his entire household, especially his son, Ishmael. The text provides no indication of the relationship
between these incidents and those that occur in Gen 18.

Genesis 18 begins with the Deity appearing to Abraham at the *'elonim*
(oaks) of Mamre, where Abraham is sitting at the opening of his tent in
the heat of the day. The text provides no clue as to exactly how long after
the circumcision incident this occurs. Thus Abraham could have been
resting while he was recuperating from his "surgery," or it could have little relationship to the previous episode. For the promise of a son by Sarah
in the next year made in 17:21 to still be true, as reaffirmed in 18:10, only
a few weeks or months could have passed between Gen 17 and Gen 18
(cf. 17:24; 21:5).

In the next verse Abraham looks up and sees three men standing near
him (18:2). As soon as Abraham sees the men, he jumps up and runs
from the entrance of the tent to greet them, bowing to the ground (18:2).
Abraham continues by asking the men not to pass their servant (Abraham; 18:3). He wants to have some water brought so they can bathe their
feet and recline under the tree (18:4). Abraham offers to fetch them bread
so they can refresh themselves (18:5). From the text it is not yet clear that
these men are messengers of the Deity. In fact, one issue in this chapter

in general is that it is not clear when the Deity is with Abraham, or if the text is referring to messengers of the Deity or the Deity in some other form (such as in Gen 17). It is also not clear whether Abraham recognizes who these people are or not.[3]

Once the visitors agree to accept the service, Abraham jumps into action. He hastens to the tent to call Sarah and tells her to make cakes (18:7). He runs to the herd to take a calf and gives it to a servant, who prepares it (18:8). He offers even more by taking curds and milk and the calf, setting them before the servants, and waiting while they eat (18:8).

Most consider this chapter, especially compared with the following Gen 19, as an example of "Oriental" hospitality. Abraham is hurrying about to prepare the feast for the visitors. He uses not regular flour but the good stuff, the choice flour used in the king's house, according to 1 Kgs 4:22, or for offerings, as in Ezek 16:13. Commentators observe that "the preparations greatly exceed the modest offer,"[4] and that "the generosity of his welcome is enhanced by his attempt to disparage his efforts."[5]

Despite Sarah's involvement in the preparation of the feast, as soon as the men are served and begin to speak, any sympathy or respect for Sarah fades from most commentaries. While eating "they," apparently one or all of the angels, say to Abraham, "Where is your wife, Sarah?" (18:9). Since Sarah is in the tent and only Abraham has gone into the tent to tell her to cook, this remark should surprise Abraham. Why should these people know the name of his wife, or care, since apparently the presence of women at such an event is not expected? Yet Abraham's response is a simple "There, in the tent" (18:9).

The next verse makes it clear that the messengers are not simply asking to be polite but that something about Sarah is directly related to their visit. "One" of the visitors (rather than "they" of 18:9) states that he "will return the next year, and your [Abraham's] wife, Sarah, shall have a son" (18:10). Interestingly enough for what will occur later, the messenger does not state who the father will be, but only that Sarah will have a son, though when the Deity speaks to Abraham in the previous chapter it is clear that Sarah would bear Abraham's son (17:16). In the same verse the text provides the detail that as the man speaks, Sarah listens at the opening of the tent that is behind him.

This verse (18:10) begins a scene where most scholars find little positive to say about Sarah. To understand what the characters are saying and the context, we need to examine the passage carefully in terms of the precise meaning of each verse and contextualize it as a block in this chapter, especially in comparison with the previous chapter. Hence, I first present a detailed discussion about what the Hebrew text states, then a discussion of how scholarship treats the episode, and finally this author's interpretation.

The narrator provides background information to what will be Sarah's response to hearing the messenger's comment: Abraham and Sarah are old and advanced in years, and Sarah has stopped having the periods of women (18:11). The placement of this verse is particularly important. Someone definitely considered it relevant for the reader to know and remember the age and status of Abraham and the status of Sarah's fertility before letting the reader know her response. If the onset of menopause for Sarah were not relevant for understanding the following comments, then this information would not have been included. But it is here to help readers understand Sarah's reaction.

Sarah's reaction is to laugh (18:12). Despite some commentators' speculations, the text does not define the nature of her laughter. Yet the text certainly does use what she says to herself to modify the laughter. Here is a fairly close translation, though not as smooth as some would like: "After I am worn-out, there will be to me joy, and my husband old!" The word for joy is *ayin-dalet-nun-he* (*'ednah*) and has the sense of "delight," also with a possible sexual connotation.[6] The simple words of her statement indicate that she thinks the visitor's announcement will come true and will bring her joy. The only possible question is whether her delight will be with her husband, who is old. Yet, there is nothing in her statement that demands reading the comment as one of disbelief that it will happen rather than pleased wonder at the news.

The following verse is what leads to the assumption that Sarah's laugh is derisive rather than one of joy. The Deity asks Abraham, "Why did Sarah laugh, saying, 'Shall I in truth bear a child, old as I am?'" (18:13). The follow-up to the Deity's statement is in the mouth, apparently, of one of the messengers: "Is anything too wonderful for the Deity? I will return to you at this time next year, and Sarah will have a son" (18:14). One of the problems with these two lines is that it is difficult to determine the difference between the Deity speaking and the Deity's messengers. Are there three messengers and the Deity all having this conversation with Abraham? Or does one messenger's words count as the Deity speaking directly? What is obviously clear is that the verse is not directed to Sarah since the sentences refer to her in the third person rather than using direct speech.

Who is speaking to whom is even more complicated in the following verse, which is not difficult to translate: "And Sarah denied/ deceived, saying, 'I did not laugh,' because she was afraid. And he said, 'No, but you laughed'" (18:15). The main thrust of the verse is clear: Sarah deceived, usually understood as "lied," saying she had not laughed, though the individual speaking to her knows that she laughed and tells her so. Sarah's reason for deceit is fear. The major questions here are the following: Who is speaking with her? Why is she lying? Ironically, we must flush out this issue before clarifying the previous verses because it is the understanding of 18:15 that governs how most interpret Sarah's actions in the earlier verses.

Most translators understand the individual speaking with Sarah in 18:15 to be the Deity.[7] Since, following this line of thought, the Deity reprimands Sarah, scholars such as von Rad can observe that "the motivation for her audacious lie ('for she was afraid') is one of those subtle psychological characteristics."[8] If Sarah's fear is not legitimate, then we cannot view anything she has said before this verse as having any merit. Furthermore, because it is the Deity who is doing the blaming, Sarah must be at fault.

Interpreting the Deity as blaming Sarah demands that all of Sarah's previous actions in this unit be viewed as negative. As a result, commentators describe Sarah as "confined, passive, cowardly, deceptive, and unfaithful."[9] Speiser defines her actions in this unit as "down-to-earth to a fault, with her curiosity, her impulsiveness, and her feeble attempt at deception."[10] Her laughter cannot be in joy but rather is "the unbelieving and perhaps somewhat evil laugh—later a work of Yahweh's was laughed at."[11] Her reaction to hearing the news "can only amuse her and she rather bluntly dismisses the matter as absurd."[12]

Modern scholarship aside, the rabbis noticed that Sarah is blamed for the same thing that Abraham does.[13] According to Darr, in the rabbis' view the reproach in 18:13 is intended *also for Abraham* since he too laughs when the Deity announces Isaac's birth (17:17).[14] The rabbis even comment that the Deity's response in 18:15 (assuming it is the Deity speaking to Sarah) is a distortion of Sarah's actions.[15] Their explanation is that Sarah's speech originally makes light of Abraham's age: "Abraham might have taken amiss what his wife had said about his advanced years and so precious is the peace between husband and wife that even the Holy One, blessed be He, preserved it at the expense of the truth."[16]

While the rabbis may have had reasons for their interpretations, they do catch something lost in many modern interpretations: Abraham *also* laughs upon hearing about the birth of Isaac. Yet, as reported in the previous chapter (above), the commentaries seldom point out the similarity in their laughter and completely ignore the difference between the reasons for the laughter. More recently, scholars are pointing out other interpretations for Sarah's actions, starting with the beginning of Genesis 18.

The text does not make the timing explicit between the arrival of the messengers (Gen 18) and the previous chapter. In Gen 17 the Deity promises Abraham a son, Isaac; then Abraham circumcises all the males of his household, including Ishmael. It cannot be long after the events of Gen 17 that the messengers arrive in Gen 18, we assume, because the Deity promises in both chapters 17 and 18 that a son would be born at the same season the following year. Yet no reason is given for the arrival of the messengers. Many assume it has to do with Gen 19, where the messengers test the people of Sodom and Gomorrah. According to Gunn and Fewell, the Deity must send a messenger because Abraham never agrees to the Deity's plan of Sarah becoming the mother of the promise.[17] Jeansonne gathers that Sarah's response to hearing the news of the birth indicates that this is the first time she has heard about the birth, though from the previous chapter the reader knows that Abraham already has heard the promise.[18] One possible reason for the messengers' stop at Abraham's tent is not just for a pause along the way to Sodom; instead, they may have the intention of directly informing Sarah of the events that would transpire. After all, Abraham has not believed the Deity's promise, is not prepared to tell her about it, and maybe is not even ready to accept its fulfillment.

Sarah's first reaction to hearing that she is going to have a child is that she is going to have joy/pleasure. Turner observes that the meaning of the term is most likely sexual pleasure.[19] If her first comment is that she will have sexual pleasure, then it means, presumably, that she and Abraham are no longer having sexual relations.[20] Informing Sarah that the couple needs to resume sexual relations would be a legitimate purpose for the messengers' trip to Abraham, especially since Abraham has not informed her of the Deity's announcement.

If we view the messengers' journey to the couple as more than a visit along the way to another event, that also legitimates Sarah's listening to the messengers' announcement. The messengers specifically ask about

Sarah's whereabouts (18:9). The messenger continues speaking, knowing that Sarah is within listening range. We must view their/his statement as showing his intention that the information he is about to offer is for Sarah's hearing. Since Abraham already knows the information he conveys, the restatement can be considered as specifically for her ears.

Sarah's response is not for public consumption. The text states clearly that Sarah laughed "to herself" (18:12). Her response contains no explicit questioning of the Deity's plans; to the contrary, her laugh expresses joy. It is only the Deity's later account of her inner speech that contains her questions about the Deity's plans. The Deity is speaking to Abraham and does not convey the interpretation directly to Sarah (18:13). The text is silent as to who else is around when the Deity has this conversation with Abraham, but the text is straightforward in portraying the conversation taking place between Abraham and the Deity. The assumption of most commentators is that the narrator and the Deity can hear humans' thoughts, and that we should consider such mind-reading as legitimate. Yet if that is the case, then the Deity would also know what Abraham is thinking when the Deity originally tells Abraham of the news (17:17). The irony is that Sarah is accused of precisely what Abraham thought upon hearing the news.

This raises the issue of who speaks to Sarah when she lies (18:15). The assumption is that the speaker who catches her lie is the Deity. Yet there are a number of reasons, both grammatical and literary, that make this scenario unlikely. First is the grammar. In 18:13 the text is quite clear that the Israelite Deity speaks directly to Abraham. As has been the problem throughout this chapter, it is not always clear if the Deity is speaking or a messenger; in either case, the text of 18:13 states that the Deity speaks with Abraham. Genesis 18:14 appears to be in the voice of one of the messengers since the verse discusses the Israelite Deity's wonder-working power and claims that the messenger will return the next year and Sarah will have a son. Then 18:15 begins with Sarah as the subject of the verb to deceive/lie, as the speaker of the phrase, "I did not laugh," and as the one who is frightened. Finally, in the last part of 18:15 we see a change in subject to a third-person-singular male speaker. This last male speaker, according to most translations and interpretations, is the messenger of the Deity. Any reader who claims that the new third-person masculine speaker is the Deity is naming the subject of the verb based on the interpretation of the verse, not on the grammar.

The problem with the Deity being the speaker in 18:15 is that the Deity has never spoken with Sarah before this and never does so later. Throughout this chapter—apparently devised so that Sarah can be informed that she will have a child with Abraham—not only do the messengers not speak to her directly; she also is hidden from everyone's sight, everyone but Abraham's. He is the only one who speaks directly to her when he gives her the order in 18:6 to make bread. Even when he is giving her instructions, he must go into the tent because she is inside of it, away from everyone's view.

Though the Deity has never spoken with Sarah, the Deity has taken care of her from the beginning. It is the Deity who saves her from Egypt after Abraham sells her into Pharaoh's harem. It is the Deity who changes Sarah's name, blesses her, and will provide her a son who will inherit the Deity's promise. In this chapter the Deity apparently sends messengers who speak specifically in her hearing, to tell her the news that Abraham neglects to convey. In the following chapters it is the Deity who will save her from Abimelech (Gen 20) and will deliver the promised son (21:1). It is the Deity who will tell Abraham to listen to Sarah and send away Hagar and Ishmael (21:12). Thus, it is hard to imagine that Sarah would fear the Deity. In fact, despite having no conversations with the Deity, Sarah brings the Deity in as judge in an earlier argument with her spouse (16:5). Finally, it is Abraham, not Sarah, whom the Deity will need to test later in the text (Gen 22).

The one whom Sarah has every right to fear is her husband, Abraham. He sells her to Pharaoh's harem. Abraham is prepared to let Hagar treat Sarah with disrespect when Hagar becomes pregnant (16:5). Though Sarah probably does not know it, Abraham also is the one who has not informed her that the Deity promises her a son, and that he has originally rejected the offer (17:18). Another thing she does not know is that her husband is the one who laughs (17:17) and does not say a word when she is blamed for what he does (18:13, 15). Therefore, it is just as plausible, in fact more likely, that Abraham is the one who says, "No, you did laugh," and that Abraham is the one whom Sarah fears.

The continuation of the chapter gives reinforcement that Abraham's guilt is at issue in Gen 18, and the messengers are testing his mettle. Here is another example of where the beginning and end of a chapter determine the theme of a chapter or unit. Most commentators and many translations include a break following 18:15. Since 18:16 begins the discussion of whether the Deity should tell Abraham about the fate of Sodom and Gomorrah, and then reports the conversation between the two, a shift makes sense. Yet the Masoretes inserted no break. When we view chapter 18 as a whole, we recognize that Abraham's actions concerning the residents of Sodom and Gomorrah—whom the narrator defines as not particularly worthy—seem awfully weak when he would not even defend his wife, who is blamed for his own actions.

Who Is Worth Saving? Genesis 18:16–33

Most commentaries consider Gen 18:16 the beginning of something new and separate it completely from the previous verses. This separation, not recognized by the Masoretes, leads scholars to comment about both the structure and content and then focus on their newly formed section. For example, Brueggemann claims that 18:16–19:38 is "loosely linked to 18:1–15 by the device of 'the men' in 18:16, 22 who in 19:1, 15 have become the 'angels/messengers,'" though even he admits that one can read "men" in both situations.[21] Once he separates the two sections he claims: "Though the two stories had no original connection, the 'men/ messengers' device is employed for placing them back to back with the theological reflection of 18:16–32 set between them."[22] Thus he first separates 18:1–15 from 18:16–19:38, without providing any reason for doing so, and then, in order to explain why they are together at all, resorts to theological explanations.

By separating the story and then determining what its theology is, Brueggemann can state: "The story (together with 18:16–32 and especially 19:29) is structured to show the tension between the *faith of Abraham* and the *waywardness of humanity*" (italics original).[23] Brueggemann is not alone in classifying the theme of the story as being rooted in praising Abraham's role in the story. Speiser also claims that the story is about how "the patriarch . . . seeks to establish for the meritorious individual the privilege of saving an otherwise worthless community."[24] The problem is that what the theology of the unit is, once the separation is imposed, is quite possibly different from what the theology, or point of the story, might have been without dividing Gen 18.

The following will consider the issues involved in the verses 18:16–33 following the Masoretic division of the text. Contrary to modern scholarship, the Masoretes saw a break at the end of Gen 18, not in its middle. According to the MT, the chapter, and presumably the same ideas or themes, continue with the men/messengers looking toward Sodom and Abraham joining them (18:16). This line is in the voice of the narrator, and the Deity wonders whether or not to hide from Abraham the Deity's intentions.

Many tie the second half of Gen 18 to the Sodom and Gomorrah scenario based on the assumption that Abraham's interest in Sodom is because of his nephew Lot. The Deity does not raise the relationship of Abraham to Lot until after the destruction of Sodom and Gomorrah (19: 29). In Gen 18 the Deity provides only one reason for discussing the situation with Abraham: "I have singled him out, that he may instruct his children and his posterity to keep the way of the LORD by doing what is just and right, in order that LORD may bring about for Abraham what He has promised" (18:19 NJPS).

The Deity then includes yet another notice that the outrage of Sodom and Gomorrah is serious (18:21).[25] This verse seems to be in the hearing of Abraham since in the next verse Abraham appears to know the Deity's intentions. Apparently still in the hearing of Abraham, the Deity decides to examine Sodom one more time (18:21). Since this verse follows the messengers' discussion with Abraham about Sarah, it seems unlikely that the messengers are only on their way to Sodom and Gomorrah and that the visit to Abraham is an added bonus. It reinforces the idea that the trip to Abraham is intentional and, from what happens during that visit, their goal for that segment of the journey seems to have been to inform Sarah of her impending pregnancy.

The next verse introduces more confusion about the separation between the messengers and the Deity: in 18:22 the men go on from there to Sodom while Abraham remains standing before the Deity. Does Abraham at this point recognize the difference between the Deity and the messengers? Regardless of what he knows about the messengers, Abraham begins defending the inhabitants of Sodom and Gomorrah by asking, "Will you sweep away the innocent along with the guilty?" (18:23 NJPS). Thus begins Abraham's bargaining with the Deity to save the cities of Sodom and Gommorah. Abraham questions the Deity's destroying the city, beginning with if there were but fifty innocent in the city (18:24), and works his way down to a mere ten innocents in the city (18:32). The Deity agrees that if ten are found, the Deity will not destroy the city (18:32). Then the Deity departs and Abraham returns to his place (18:33).

Commentators traditionally stress that Abraham's discussion with the Deity shows his righteousness: he even challenges his Deity to protect innocent inhabitants.[26] This stands out boldly when 18:16–33 is paired with the following chapter. The Masoretes did not make this connection. Instead, they coupled the second half of Gen 18 with the first half. Genesis 18:1–15 indicates that Abraham has not informed his wife, Sarah, of the Deity's promise to him in 17:15–21, that she will be the mother of nations. Regardless of who is speaking to Sarah in 18:15, Abraham does not stand up to the Deity or the messengers for the sake of his own wife. In Gen 19 the Deity destroys the cities of Sodom and Gomorrah, presumably confirming the Deity's original analysis that the towns are not worth saving. The lack of ten innocent individuals in Sodom and Gomorrah and the towns' destruction by the Deity, prove that Abraham's efforts are misguided since the Deity does not discover even ten innocent individuals in the towns. This means that Abraham uses his clout with the Deity—his big battle for justice—not for his wife but for a town's inhabitants who are not deserving of his defense. On a broad theological plain the idea of standing up to protect the righteous over the wicked seems noble, and yet Abraham chooses a poor case. While this analysis may seem harsh, Gen. 20 reinforces this view of Abraham's poor sense of judgment: Abraham does the opposite at Gerar, assuming the worst about a town and its king, only to be proved wrong.

The Destruction of Sodom and Gomorrah: Genesis 19

The MT separates Gen 19 from both Gen 18 and Gen 20. Since the focus of this volume is on Sarah and her relationship with Abraham, and neither appears in Gen 19, there is no need for us to cover Gen 19 in detail. But the chapter does fall between two important episodes in Abraham's career. Genesis 19 deserves some attention because it proves the futility of Abraham's fight for the people of Sodom and Gomorrah and contrasts sharply with his treatment of the king of Gerar in Gen 20. Hence, I will examine Gen 19 here with Gen 18 because most modern scholars treat it that way. We will not study it in detail but only the elements that impact Abraham, the interpretation of his actions, what is to follow, and how different Gen 18 is when it is separated from Gen 19.

At the end of 18:22 the Deity finishes speaking with Abraham, who returns "to his place." Genesis 19 begins by focusing on two men/messengers, though three of them have been visiting Abraham to this point. When they arrive in Sodom, Lot is there to meet them and urges them to go to his house to spend the night; this is different from Gen 18, where they show up at the entrance to Abraham's tent. The men/messengers readily accept Abraham's invitation to dine with him, but at Sodom they do not immediately accept Lot's invitation. This could reflect a difference in the hospitality offered or further proof that the intention of the messengers in Gen 18 is to convey information to Sarah about the birth of Isaac, whereas in their visit to Sodom they have a quite different mission.

The men/messengers return to Lot's house, and he prepares a feast for them (19:3). Before they have a chance to lie down, the people of Sodom surround the house (19:4) and demand that Lot send out the messengers so that they may be intimate with them (19:5). Lot protests, offering his own daughters (19:6–8), who are of no interest to the men of Sodom (19:9). As Lot is about to be attacked by the crowd the men/messengers save him (19:10), using a blinding light so that the crowd cannot find the door to the house (19:11). The men's use of special power to protect Lot is more definitive of their divine status than anything that happens in their encounters with Abraham and Sarah.

The men/messengers encourage Lot to bring out any other relatives that he wants to be saved from the city because the Deity is going to destroy the place (19:12). Lot's sons-in-law meet this warning with derision (19:13–14). At dawn Lot still has not left the city, and the men/messengers urge him to take his wife and remaining daughters and leave (19:15). Even this does not work; the men/messengers take the hands of Lot, his wife, and two daughters and bring him outside the city (19:15–16), telling him to flee for his life and not to look behind or stop in the plain lest they be swept away (19:17). Lot is still not paying attention and suggests that he flee to a nearby town instead (19:20), to which the men/messengers acquiesce (19:21); they still insist that he hurry (19:22). In this segment it is clear that Lot is trying to follow the directions of the men/messengers, appreciates what they are doing for him, and yet cannot grasp the enormity of what is happening. In Lot's defense, there is no indication that Lot was ever in contact with the Israelite Deity. Despite the problems he has in Sodom earlier (14:12–16), he is not aware of the Deity's feelings toward the city. At the same time, Lot does take care to try to save the rest of his family in the city and appears to act quickly in relaying to them the information he has received—which is more than his uncle Abraham does with his wife in this story line.

Lot apparently leaves just in time. As the sun rises and Lot enters

Zoar, the Deity rains some sort of fire upon Sodom and Gomorrah from heaven (19:24), thereby annihilating the cities and the entire plain and all the inhabitants of the cities, even the vegetation (19:25).[27] At this point Lot's wife looks back and turns into a pillar of salt (19:26). Now Abraham reappears in the story. Early that very morning Abraham returns to the place where he had stood before the Deity for their last conversation the day before, looks down toward Sodom and Gomorrah, and sees the smoke of the land rising as from a furnace (19:28). The text does not say anything about Abraham's emotions upon seeing the destruction. It also does not state whether Abraham knows that Lot is saved, or whether the Deity tells him about Lot's status. In the next verse the narrator explains that when the Deity destroys the cities of the plain where Lot dwells, the Deity is mindful of Abraham and therefore removes Lot from the destruction (19:29). Again, there is no report that the Deity conveys this information to Abraham in any way. From the story of Gen 18–19, it would appear to Abraham that the Deity has not found even ten innocent individuals and that Lot and his family are destroyed with the rest of the inhabitants.

The following verses do not clarify the situation, but could be considered further proof that Abraham does not know of Lot's rescue. Following the destruction Lot goes up from Zoar and settles in the hill country with his two daughters in a cave (19:30). The text does not explain precisely where this "hill country" is compared to where Abraham is dwelling at the time. The fact that Lot's family lives in a cave and the daughters think that there are no men left for them indicates that they do not have much contact with anyone, certainly not those of Lot's uncle's household (19:31). In this episode they take turns getting their father drunk and having sexual relations with him so that they may conceive and maintain life through their father (19:33–35). The daughters then give birth to two children, Moab and Ammon, both of whom father nations—Moabites and Ammonites—that later become enemies of Israel (19:37–38).

One could comment at length on the daughters' actions and the birth of their children, but they are not relevant for the purposes of this study. What is significant here is that these are the last few verses before Sarah and Abraham's trip to Gerar, where Abraham will again give his wife to another man with the possibility that sexual intercourse could take place between them. Most discussions of the episode focus on whether Lot's daughters are right or wrong to have sex with their father, and what this says about Lot and the future enemies of Israel. Commentators consistently neglect the relationship between the accounts of Lot's daughters and Abraham's trek to Gerar and what this might mean. Nevertheless, the text presents the account of Lot's escape from Sodom and cohabiting with his daughters by sandwiching it between the announcement that Sarah and Abraham will have a child, and an episode where Abraham gives his wife to another man. Abraham's actions, which we will discuss in more detail in the following chapter, are particularly suspect in Gerar since the Deity has just told him that he will father a child with Sarah. The final issue raised in Gen 19 is not about the innocence or righteousness of the citizens of Sodom, but on some levels the question of who should father a child, with whom, and under what circumstances. Speiser comments that the daughters think they are the last people on earth and the father is not a conscious party to the encounter. Hence, "all of this adds up to praise rather than blame."[28] Is it possible that the same can be said for Sarah and Abraham in the following chapter?

Conclusions

I maintain that we should consider all of Gen 18 as a unified whole and not as a sidebar to Gen 19. Then Gen 18 no longer functions as a prelude to the Sodom discussion, with an Abrahamic element added to relate it to the entire narrative of Gen 18 and Gen 19. The messengers visit to Abraham is intentional, not an added bonus to the Sodom episode. Sarah does not accidentally eavesdrop on the discussion of the messengers: the goal of their visit is to make sure that she overhears that she will bear a son to Abraham. The grammar and other data in the text do not support the long-held notion that the Deity accuses Sarah of lying. Once we have dismantled this argument, it becomes clear that Sarah does not fear the Deity but her husband, Abraham. After not standing up for his wife about something he himself does (laughing at the Deity's promise of a son), Abraham uses his prestige and clout with the Deity to protect towns that Gen 19 proves are not worth saving. The final incident in Gen 19 concerns the sexual encounter between Lot and his daughters, raising the issue of who are legitimate sexual partners, especially in extreme contexts. All of this information lays the groundwork for issues that are the central concern in the following chapter, Gen 20, which lays the groundwork for the birth of Isaac, the banishment of Ishmael, and the binding or sacrifice of Isaac.

Notes

1. For example, E. A. Speiser, *Genesis* (Anchor Bible 1; Garden City, N.Y.: Doubleday, 1985), 128–35, G. von Rad, *Genesis: A Commentary* (Old Testament Library; Philadelphia: Westminster, 1972), 203–9, who actually considers the break to be after Gen 18:16.

2. W. Brueggemann, *Genesis* (Interpretation; Atlanta: John Knox, 1982), 162–77, D. W. Cotter, *Genesis* (Berit Olam; Collegeville: Liturgical Press, 2003), 116–17, treats Gen 18:1–19:38 as essentially one block of text.

3. Speiser observes that the Hebrew consonants can represent "my lord" (singular), "my lords" (ordinary plural), or the special form with the long third vowel that is reserved for the Deity: "my/the Lord." Speiser, *Genesis*, 129.

4. Von Rad, *Genesis*, 206.

5. Speiser, *Genesis*, 131.

6. BDB, 726.

7. For example, NJPS translates "He," capitalizing the *h* to indicate that the Deity is speaking to Sarah. Even R. E. Friedman's new translation capitalizes "He," assuming the Deity to be the speaker. R. E. Friedman, *Commentary on the Torah* (San Francisco: HarperSanFrancisco, 2001), 64.

8. Von Rad, *Genesis*, 207.

9. E. Fuchs, "The Literary Characterization of Mothers and Sexual Politics in the Hebrew Bible," in *Feminist Perspectives on Biblical Scholarship* (ed. A. Yarbro Collins; Atlanta: Scholars Press, 1985), 117–36.

10. Speiser, *Genesis*, 131.

11. Von Rad, *Genesis*, 207.

12. Ibid.

13. K. Pfisterer Darr, "More Than the Stars of the Heavens: Critical, Rabbinical, and Feminist Perspectives on Sarah," in *Far More Precious Than Jewels: Perspectives on Biblical Women* (Gender and the Biblical Tradition; Louisville: Westminster/John Knox Press, 1991), 103.

14. Ibid.

15. Ibid.

16. Ibid.

17. Dana Fewell and David Gunn, *Gender Power and Promise* (Nashville: Abingdon, 1993).

18. S. Pace Jeansonne, *The Women of Genesis* (Minneapolis: Fortress, 1990), 25.

19. L. A. Turner, *Announcement of Plot in Genesis* (JSOTSup 96; Sheffield: JSOT Press, 1990), 79.

20. Ibid.

21. Brueggemann, *Genesis*, 162

22. Ibid.

23. Ibid., 163.

24. Speiser, *Genesis*, 135.

25. The text has previously stated that Sodom is problematic (Gen 13:13).

26. Speiser, *Genesis*, 135; Brueggemann, *Genesis*, 168.

27. The text does not clarify the final status of Zoar. The small town is saved so that Lot and his daughters find refuge there in 19:23. The text provides no reason for Lot to leave Zoar in 19:30 and settle in the hill country. Lot's daughters later comment that there are "no men on earth for them to sleep with" (19:31), which may indicate that Zoar was destroyed, or the daughters thought it was.

28. Speiser, *Genesis*, 145.

CHAPTER 5

The Evolving Family: Genesis 20–22

Immediately following the destruction of Sodom and Gomorrah, Abraham takes Sarah to Gerar in the Negev. This sharp break between the end of Gen 19 and Gen 20 appears in the commentaries of modern scholarship, the MT, and will be followed here. Despite the break between Gen 19 and Gen 20, certain issues stand out in Gen 18 when it is read as one complete chapter. These issues focus not so much on Abraham and his relationship to Sodom, as between Abraham and whom he chooses to protect. Hence, it now is much easier to see those issues as they appear in Gen 20.

Many examinations of Gen 20 focus on the similarities and differences between the so-called wife-sister stories found in Gen 12:10–20, chapter 20, and even 26:1–11. This examination will touch upon some of those issues, insofar as they are relevant for the major focus of this volume: the role of Sarah and the relationship among her, Abraham, and the Israelite Deity. Because of the larger theme of this study, we must also pay attention to Abraham's reasons for going to Gerar and handing over his wife, how he handles the king of Gerar's accusations, his final actions to correct the situation, and their impact on Sarah and the Deity's promise of an heir.

Genesis 20 neatly relates to issues raised in Gen 18 and 19 and also serves as a transition to the result of Abraham's actions in those stories: the Deity's need to test him. Genesis 20 serves as a bridge between Gen

18–19 and the issues (in Gen 20–22) surrounding Isaac's birth, the exile of Ishmael, and the sacrifice of Isaac. In some of these stories Sarah is an active player; in others she does not appear. As throughout this study, even when Sarah is not an active player, the themes and issues raised by Abraham and his actions impact both her role and her status within the story and the book, and therefore we must consider the larger scene.

This chapter examines Gen 20–22 because of the themes raised here that tie all three chapters together.

Why the Negev and Why Now?

Genesis 19 ends with the birth of Lot's daughter's sons, who become the "fathers" of the Moabites and Ammonites (19:37–38). Suddenly in Gen 20:1 Abraham is traveling to the land of the Negev. The shift is rather abrupt.[1] There is little in the content of the two episodes that demands any connection, though in light of the themes raised in the previous chapter about the focus of Gen 18, there may be more connection then is generally perceived.

The phrasing and ensuing wife-sister story instead connect with Abram's earlier journey to Egypt. Although Gen 12:9 is not traditionally part of the wife-sister story of 12:10–20, it also has Abram traveling to the Negev. Both 12:9 and 20:1 use the same verb "to journey": *yod-samekh-ayin* (*yisaʿ*), from *nun-samek-ayin* (*nasaʿ*). In both cases he is traveling to the Negev, in 12:9 "by stages," here simply to the "land of the Negev." In Gen 12 the Negev is not his final destination: only when they arrive in Egypt does Abram hand Sarah over to Pharaoh's house (12:15). Here Abraham travels no farther than Gerar (20:1).

Another significant difference between Gen 12 and 20 is that Gen 20 provides no reason for Abraham's travels.[2] In Gen 12 the text states that there is a severe famine in the land (12:10). In analyzing Gen 12 we discussed whether it is appropriate for Abram to leave the land because of the famine, but at least the text provides a reason for his actions. Here the text provides none. Because of the juxtaposition of Gen 19 with Gen 20, one may wonder whether Abraham leaves where he has "settled" at Mamre, just north of Hebron (13:18; 18:1), because of the destruction he sees in Gen 19. The text does not indicate whether Abraham knows that Lot and his daughters have survived the catastrophe.

As with Gen 18, the text provides no hints about the timing of the events. The announcements of a child for Sarah, recorded in 17:21 and 18:14, say that a year hence Sarah will have a child. In 21:2 Sarah has the child at the promised time, as the text claims. Hence, the story line allows only a few weeks or months between the announcement of the impending birth and the events about to transpire in Gerar.

Abraham travels to the Negev, and the text adds that he settles between Kadesh and Shur, and also for a time becomes a resident alien in Gerar (20:1). This Kadesh is likely Kadesh-barnea (and Kedesh south of Judah, Josh 15:23; but not Kedesh in Galilee).[3] It is in the northern Sinai, where the Israelites would camp before entering the land of Canaan, and thus must be outside the boundary of Canaan.[4] Shur is a desert region of the northern Sinai between the southern border of Canaan and the northeast border of Egypt, and like Kadesh, is outside Canaan.[5] It also happens to be the area to which Hagar flees and finds a well (16:7, 14; and where Isaac will live; 24:62). Ironically, when the Israelites are in the desert following their exodus from Egypt, they also wander into the wilderness of Shur. They find no water until the Deity miraculously sweetens the bitter water at Marah and Israel finds twelve springs of water at Elim (Exod 15:22–27). Gerar is a town in the western Negev, likely identified with Tell Haror.[6] In Genesis, the town is used as a marker of the southern border of Canaan (10:19).[7] Two of the other sites used as marking the southern border of Canaan in the same reference are Sodom and Gomorrah. What is less clear is if the southern border is considered part of Canaan or just at its edge.

According to Speiser there is a geographical problem since Gerar is not located between Kadesh and Shur.[8] Because of this problem Speiser and others translate Gen 20:1 as follows: "Abraham journeyed on to the region of the Negev and settled between Kadesh and Shur. While he was sojourning in Gerar"—and then continue into 20:2.[9] The difference may not be significant, but the Masoretes place an end to the sentence following the reference to residence in Gerar. Thus, the translation should be the following: "Abraham journeyed from there to the land of the Negev, and he settled between Kadesh and Shur. And he became a resident alien in Gerar." While Speiser's translation solves the geography issue, it means the reference to Abraham's being in Gerar is background to what he says to Sarah. In the Masoretes' understanding of the verse, however, Abraham's stay in Gerar is the final destination of the clan and the climax of the sentence, rather than being simply part of an adverbial phrase. Since the role of Gerar is important for all of Gen 20, a good portion of Gen 21, and even later with Isaac (Gen 26), it seems preferable to follow the Masoretic division of the text and see Gerar as a destination for Abraham.

If such is the case, then the geographical problem of Gerar not being between Kadesh and Shur still exists. One possible solution is that the geography provided by the biblical text in general is loose. Gerar may not be between the two points mentioned, but it is certainly in that general area, south and west of where Abraham is earlier (at Mamre, near Hebron). There may be other reasons for the text to list these place names, reasons showing less concern for drawing a map than for indicating a shift, or possibly continuing a focus of Abraham's interest. Shur is the direction that Hagar was heading when she runs away and is informed of Ishmael's birth (16:7). For the rest of Abraham's life, with the exception of going to Hebron to buy a burial plot for Sarah when she dies, Abraham lives in the region of the Negev and Beer-sheba. Genesis 21:21 has Ishmael living in the wilderness of Paran, which is just south of Kadesh-barnea, west of Edom, north of the wilderness of Sinai, and thus near Abraham's range between Kadesh and Shur (20:1).[10] In fact, Num 13:26 reports that the spies return to Kadesh, a town on the north edge of the wilderness of Paran. If the identification of Kadesh-barnea with Tell el-Qudeirat is correct, then Kadesh is located near the junctures of the Way to Shur, a branch from the Via Maris (a major route along the Mediterranean), and the Way to the Arabah.[11] Hence, Abraham situates himself closer to Egypt and will remain in this area, close to where his son Ishmael settles. Again, whether this is coincidence or intentional is pure speculation. At this point in the story Ishmael is not an adult, has not been exiled from Abraham's household, and is not yet married to an Egyptian woman, but it may become an important factor later when all of these events transpire.

What is clear about Abraham's location is that he has moved to a different part of the country, with no reason provided by the text. Does he need a change of pace? Is it too distressing to see the destroyed cities of the plain? Is he trying to avoid the Deity's messengers since he is about to show no sign of trying to fulfill the Deity's promise of a son through Sarah? It is not clear, and the text does nothing to help the reader fill in the blanks.

The text continues with Abraham saying that "his wife Sarah" is his sister; the text does not state whom he tells (20:2). This leads to a situation similar to what happened in Egypt. King Abimelech of Gerar sends and takes Sarah (20:2).[12] There are clear parallels here with what happens in Gen 12, but also significant differences. The text provides no reason for Abraham's entrance into the region and putting his wife in harm's way again. Rashkow comments: "Unless Abraham's material gain is considered a motive, Abraham's exploitation of Sarah a second time is unfathomable. . . . Abraham does not claim to fear being killed because of Sarah's beauty as he did when he approached Egypt, which casts doubts upon his later rationale to Abimelech."[13] Ironically, commentators like von Rad feel that this affair is less offensive because it is presented so tersely and is somewhat ameliorated—in von Rad's estimate of the narrator's opinion—because Sarah really was Abraham's sister (see below).[14]

As opposed to the situation in Egypt, this time there is every reason in the world for Abraham to go out of his way to protect Sarah from falling into the wrong hands, or bed, in this case: the Deity just promised him a child through her.[15] The lack of a specified motive for going to Gerar in the first place, combined with Abraham's quick claim to kinship as opposed to marriage, makes this case much more shocking. It is also possible to claim, though unlikely, that Abraham does not know what would happen to Sarah in Egypt; but after he has turned her over once, he must now have a good idea what could happen to her. His quick decision to let Abimelech take her indicates that, in his mind, the benefits of turning his wife over to the leader of a foreign land far outweigh any risks or negative results. The last time he became rich (in Egypt); maybe the same will happen again. According to Turner, either Abraham does not believe that the Deity is going to grant him another son through Sarah, or he prefers Ishmael, or he wants to make Sarah's son unacceptable because it would be Abimelech's seed.[16] Another option is that Abraham is testing the Deity. What better way to make the Deity prove the Deity's powers than by placing his wife in another's bed?

Ironically, Abimelech will claim not to have touched her, and the Deity will verify it; so in this case the text is more straightforward about the reason for Abimelech taking Sarah. In the Egyptian episode, Pharaoh's people saw her and had her taken to his house, using the passive of the verb "to take" (12:15). The verb "to take" can have sexual connotations, and by placing it in the passive voice, the text is unclear about the intent in that case. The Gerar situation is different. The text claims that King Abimelech sends (his people) and takes her (20:2). Even in the biblical text sometimes the term "to take" means just "to take," and in this case Abimelech never has the chance to take her sexually. But the language is more straightforward than in 12:15, meaning that Abimelech instigated the taking.

The text now focuses on Abimelech. "Elohim" (God, a suitable term for the Deity since Abimelech does not know the proper name of Abraham's Deity) comes to Abimelech in a dream by night, tells him that he will die because of the woman he has taken, and that she is a married woman (20:3). Sarah's married state is referred to as her being the "owner of an owner" (*b' 'ulat ba'al*), though it is usually translated as "a man's wife." This expression is rarely used and, according to Rashkow, primarily in negative situations.[17] Does it depict Sarah as powerless, turning her into a possession, or does it reveal that because she possesses a possessor she should be protected? In either case she is clearly not being treated the way a woman in such a context should be; otherwise the Deity would not have to step in again to protect her.

The narrator then informs the reader that Abimelech has not approached her (Sarah) sexually (20:4). Nothing in the text suggests that he lacks an intention to approach her sometime, but at this point he has not yet done so. This is important for the story line because 21:2 contains the news that Sarah conceives and bears a son, and the text is explicit that the father is Abraham. Alexander picks up Westermann's observation that Gen 20 displays a special interest in the issue of guilt; they associate it with the account's theological reflection in 12:10–13:1. Alexander emphasizes that they overlook the issue of the paternity of Isaac if Abimelech's innocence is not completely clear.[18]

The narrator's statement in 20:4 confirms Abimelech's next statement, which otherwise could be questioned. Abimelech, likely still in his dream, questions whether "my Lord" (*'adonai*, an address of respect; not the proper name of Abraham's Deity) will slay people even though innocent (20:4). The king claims that Abraham himself said, "She is my sister," and that she said, "He is my brother." Abimelech swears that his heart is blameless and his hands are clean (20:5).

Abimelech's reference to slaying the innocent is especially powerful in light of Abraham's recent discussions with the Deity in Gen 18, when compared to his actions in this chapter. In 18:23–32 Abraham goes out of his way to argue for the theoretical innocents of Sodom, whose residents the text has already recognized as somehow "bad" (Gen 13:13), and which Abraham has already saved once (Gen 14). The Deity agrees to Abraham's terms, sends messengers to find enough righteous individuals to save the city, but does not find them (Gen 19). In this next chapter Abraham, providing no reason (he will later), leads Abimelech astray, as he does Pharaoh earlier. Abraham eventually gives his reasons for the kinship claim (evaluated below). Regardless of whether Abraham and Sarah are in any way brother and sister, they are definitely husband and

wife, and therefore Abraham had deleted a significant piece of information that would govern Abimelech's conduct. In this case Abraham's
actions are even more egregious because it follows an incident where
Abraham is prepared to assume the best about the people of Sodom, and
yet here he assumes the worst about Abimelech. Not only is Abraham
making assumptions about the actions of the ruler of Gerar; he is also
prepared to place his wife in danger because of them. The timing of this
is a mere two chapters after he is prepared to let Sarah suffer for actions
he himself commits (laughing; 17:17; 18:12–15). Again, following the
pattern as in Egypt, the Israelite Deity (or Elohim) must protect foreign
rulers and Sarah from Abraham.

Elohim, as in the case of Sodom and Gomorrah, is prepared to protect the innocent. In 21:6 Elohim, still in the dream, tells Abimelech that
Elohim knows he is blameless, has kept Abimelech from sinning against
Elohim, and kept him from touching Sarah. This is further verification
that Abimelech's intention was to touch Sarah sexually. Since the Deity
knows this and Abimelech intends it, surely also Abraham suspects it
could happen.

Although the Deity keeps disaster from happening, Abimelech still
has to correct the situation. The Deity informs Abimelech that he needs
to restore the man's wife, and tells him that Abraham is a prophet, who
will intercede for him to save Abimelech's life (20:7). Furthermore, if
Abimelech does not restore Sarah, he will die, he and all that is his. Even
though Abimelech has done nothing wrong, according to Abimelech and
the Israelite Deity, to extricate himself from the situation he still has work
to do.

Abimelech takes the Deity's warning seriously and the next morning
calls his servants and tells them what happened, which frightens them
(20:8). Abimelech then calls Abraham, asking, "What did you do to us?"
(20:9)—quite similar to Pharaoh's question to Abram (12:18). Abimelech
charges Abraham with bringing upon Abimelech's kingdom a great "sin"
(*chet-tet-alef-he* = *chata'ah*, 20:9) and asks what reason he has for doing
such a thing (20:10). Similar to the situation with Pharaoh, Abraham
endangers their houses, assuming a danger without any evidence for it, a
danger both rulers seemingly deny by their gifts to him.

Abraham's response emphasizes connecting Gen 20 with Gen 18 because Abraham claims, "I thought, There is no fear of the Lord in this
place, and they will kill me because of my wife" (20:11).[19] The irony is
profound. Abimelech tells Abraham that he has caused a great sin to fall
upon his city, precisely why the Israelite Deity destroys Sodom and

Gomorrah, because of their great sin (18:20). In the Sodom and Gomorrah situation, Abraham argues with the Deity about saving the city based
on a mere ten innocent individuals, who did not exist. In the next story
Abraham assumes a lack of fear of his Deity (20:11) that almost causes a
great sin to be committed by the ruler and his entire city. Again, Abraham
is wrong. Both incidents follow immediately upon Abraham's wife being
accused of something Abraham does, and Abraham does not come to her
rescue. In all three cases the Israelite Deity must correct the situation.

Abraham's response to Abimelech also includes a justification for his
action beyond his poor judgment; he claims that Sarah is in truth his sister since they share the same father, though not the same mother
(20:12). He even embellishes it further by claiming that his Deity made
him wander from his father's house, and so Abraham asked her, as a
kindness to him, that whenever they come to a new place she will say,
"He is my brother" (20:13). At this point interpreters bring comparisons
with Gen 12 and differences in authors into the discussions of this chapter, as well as the possible legitimacy of Abraham's statement.[20] There
may be some validity to the suggestion that nothing in the biblical text
says the reader must believe Abraham. Abraham is wrong about Sarah's
laughter, he is wrong about finding ten innocents in Sodom and Gomorrah, and he is wrong in his assumption of what Abimelech now, and
Pharaoh earlier, would do if they knew Abraham and Sarah were married. There is no record of a conversation between Abraham and Sarah
where he instructs her *always* to say that she is his sister, only the one
conversation upon their entry to Egypt, when Sarai does not speak
(12:11–13). According to Jeansonne, neither the narrator nor any other
dialogue or genealogical source confirms the statement that Abraham
and Sarah were half brother and half sister.[21] The narrator implies that
the reader can doubt Abraham's veracity because he lies a number of
times.[22] There would be no point for the genealogy of Terah's family in
11:24–30 if it does not mention such an important familial relationship.
That record names a father for Milcah, Abram's brother Nahor's wife,
but none for Sarah (11:29–30). Finally, the similar story in Egypt gives
no hint of any veracity to a brother-sister relationship when Abram
broaches the subject with Sarai (12:11–13), carries it out (12:14–15), or
is questioned about it afterward by Pharaoh (12:18–19). This late in the
story, with so many poor calls by Abraham in a number of different stories, it is hard to imagine that the narrator wants the reader to view
Abraham's response as one to be accepted without question.

Even if there were any truth to Abraham's story, it would not considerably change what he has done, his intentions, or the result of his actions. Abraham's Deity tells him that he will have a son through his wife, Sarah (17:16, 21; 18:10, 14), and almost immediately he gives her to a foreign ruler (20:2). Abraham tells the ruler that they are brother and sister rather than married, leading the ruler to take her into his household, clearly with the intention of having a sexual union with her. The result of Abimelech's action is to put himself and his entire kingdom at risk (20:3–4, 7, 9, 17–18). Abimelech now has to depend upon Abraham to undo what is set in motion by Abraham's actions. Thus, regardless of the veracity of Abraham's kinship to Sarah, his neglect to inform Abimelech of their marriage leads to the problems Abimelech faces.

The result of the situation, like that in Egypt, is that Abraham becomes wealthy. In this instance Abimelech takes sheep and oxen and male and female slaves and gives them to Abraham (20:14).[23] Abimelech restores Sarah to Abraham, thereby protecting the Deity's promise (20:14). Abimelech even offers Abraham land, telling him that he can settle wherever he pleases (20:15). Not only does Abimelech settle with Abraham; he also provides Sarah's "brother" with a thousand pieces of silver (20:16). Although the Hebrew text is not completely straightforward, the silver seems to be compensation that helps to clear Sarah's reputation. The money will induce people to overlook the injury done to Sarah and let them know that she is vindicated (20:17).[24]

Once Abimelech suitably pays off Abraham and Sarah's name is cleared, Abraham takes action. Genesis 20:18 informs the reader that the Deity has closed the wombs of the household of Abimelech because of Sarah, the wife of Abraham. Ironically, that information is imparted only after Abraham prays to the Deity, who heals Abimelech and his wife and his slave-girls so that they bear children (20:17).

The reference to Abraham praying ties in neatly with the Deity's earlier statement that Abraham is a prophet (20:7) and can intercede in Abimelech's behalf. Scholars have trouble with the reference to Abraham as a prophet: they usually do not consider the idea of a prophet with special oracular powers happening this early in biblical chronology. Speiser treats the reference not as meaning one with special oracular powers but "one who speaks out," on behalf of another.[25] At the time the Deity makes the pronouncement, it seems to function as reinforcement in persuading Abimelech to let Abraham go and return his wife to him, because Abraham will someday be able to do something for him. At that point the text does not mention the womb-closing problem caused by Abimelech's taking Sarah. Only at the end of the chapter, after it has been fixed, is the situation revealed. It is odd that this is the first time the text mentions Abraham's prophetic qualities, whatever they may be, and also the first time that Abraham prays on behalf of anybody other than himself. Thus far he has offered sacrifices to the Deity, circumcised his household in line with the Deity's commands, and made requests of the Deity, usually for himself but also for Ishmael and the theoretical innocents of Sodom and Gomorrah, but never for anyone else.

The chapter finishes with most of the loose ends tied up, possibly more so than at first glance. Abraham is richer than before and now has received the right to dwell in the region with the ruler's blessing. Abraham's wife, Sarah, has been restored to him. This last information becomes particularly important in the next chapter. Sarah's ability to give birth may have more to do with the Abimelech episode than readers usually grant. The text says that Abraham prays to the Deity, who heals Abimelech and his wife and slave girls (20:17). At this point Sarah has only just been restored to Abraham (20:14). Might Sarah have benefited from Abraham's prayer? Not only has Abraham never prayed on anyone's behalf before this in the story; he also has never even asked the Deity for a child on Sarah's behalf. The Deity's pronouncement that Sarah would have a child is based on the Deity's decision. Another parallel is the situation with Isaac and Rebekah, who also is barren. Isaac pleads on her behalf, and she becomes pregnant (25:21). Regardless of the relationship between Abraham's prayer and Sarah's stay with Abimelech, in the next chapter the Deity's promise that Sarah will bear a child is fulfilled.

The Birth of Isaac

Genesis 21:1 begins a new chapter, according to modern scholarship and the Masoretes, by finally introducing Isaac. The text recounts how the Deity takes note of Sarah, following the Deity's promise, and does for Sarah as the Deity has said (21:1). The Deity gives the promise of Sarah's child directly to Abraham (17:16, 21; 18:10) and through the messengers lets Sarah overhear (18:10) the news, but 21:1 mentions only Sarah. The emphasis on Sarah, after the Deity has promised this for Sarah, reinforces the notion that one of the main goals of the three messengers' trip to visit Abraham and Sarah in Gen 18 is to inform Sarah about the pending birth of a son.

Despite chapters of discussion about the birth that will happen, Isaac's conception and delivery occurs in a mere one verse. Genesis 21:2 reports that Sarah conceives and bears a son to Abraham in his old age, and confirms that it all happened when the Deity said it would. The next verse has Abraham giving his son the name Isaac and affirms Isaac as the one whom Sarah had borne to him (21:3). When the child is eight days old, Abraham circumcises him, as the Israelite Deity has commanded (21:4). The narrator then reminds readers that Abraham is a hundred years old when his son Isaac is born to him (21:5). In only five verses Isaac is conceived by, born to, and named and circumcised by elderly parents.

Genesis 21:6 continues with the idea of 21:1, that this is done for Sarah. The text tells nothing about Abraham's personal feelings or attitude toward the event, only his action of naming and circumcising the child. Such is not the case with Sarah, who claims, "Elohim has made laughter for me. All who hear will laugh for me."[26] She adds, "Who would say to Abraham, 'Sarah will suckle sons'? But I have borne a son for his old age" (21:7). My fairly literal translation captures the idea that Sarah is thrilled with the joyous news. Jeansonne observes that these first seven verses mention Sarah's name six times; thus, we should read her response as one of joy and personal triumph.[27] According to Jeansonne, Sarah's words imply that no one will be able to deride her for being childless and indicate that she understands the incredible reality of her being able to give birth.[28]

Yet not all read Sarah's comments as those of happiness and awe. The RSV translates, "God has made laughter for me; everyone who hears will laugh over me" (21:6). The idea of laughing "over" someone is not necessarily a positive image. Von Rad translates the verse and is more explicit about his understanding of Sarah's laughter: "God has made laughter for me, every one who hears will laugh over me" (21:6). "In v. 6 there are two very different statements. The first speaks in the sense of devout thanksgiving of a laugh of joy which God gave to the sterile woman. The other (v. 6b), apparently with reference to ch 18:12, thinks in embarrassment of the laughter and talk that will now take place among the neighbors."[29] In Alter's view, "The ambiguity of both the noun ('laughter') and the accompanying preposition ('to' or 'for' or 'with' or 'at me') is wonderfully suited to the complexity of the moment. It may be laughter, triumphant joy, that Sarah experiences and that is the name of the child Isaac ('he-who-laughs'). But in her very exultation she may feel the absurdity."[30] This may be yet another case where much of how one views Sarah's laughter depends on how one considers Sarah's earlier actions. Regardless of one's attitude toward Sarah, Gen 21 makes it clear that the Deity is fulfilling the Deity's promise to Sarah, and that Sarah is the one expressing joy about the birth. All we know of Abraham is that he is accomplishing the ritual actions that go with the birth of a son. The text provides no insight into Abraham's feelings or emotions concerning the birth of his son Isaac.

The text again fast-forwards through Isaac's early years, and suddenly in Gen 21:8 Abraham is throwing a feast for the day Isaac is weaned. The text does not make clear the relationship between the weaning feast and the following verses, where Sarah becomes outraged at Ishmael. Did something associated with the weaning of Isaac or the feast held to commemorate that event cause the following actions, or are they to be considered completely separate events? Von Rad claims that children were weaned at about three years of age in ancient Israel (citing 1 Sam 1:23; 2 Macc 7:27), and from then on began a new period in the child's life.[31] The text's juxtaposition of the feast with the following banishment of Ishmael could mean that the feast and what it symbolizes cause Sarah to consider the relationship between Ishmael and Isaac in a new light because of Isaac's new situation. The relationship of 21:8 to 21:9 will become clearer when reviewing various translations of 21:9.

According to 21:9, "Sarah saw the son of Hagar the Egyptian, whom she bore to Abraham, playing" (MT). To understand why there is so much controversy over the word "playing" (*m' tsacheq*, Piel participle of *tsachaq*), the result of that action must be considered. The "playing" encounter leads Sarah to tell Abraham, "Send out this slave woman and her son because the son of this slave woman will not inherit with my son, with Isaac" (21:10). The implication seems to be that the action of "playing" causes Sarah to demand a drastic measure from Abraham.

A few translations reveal the issue. The NJPS begins a new paragraph after 21:9: "Sarah saw the son whom Hagar the Egyptian had borne to Abraham playing." Though the RSV understands the action to be "playing," it differs by considering 21:10 in the same paragraph with 21:9: "But Sarah saw the son of Hagar the Egyptian, whom she had borne to Abraham, playing with her son Isaac" ("with her son Isaac" is in LXX and Vulgate, not in MT). The KJV and NJPS agree to begin a new paragraph with 21:10, but KJV translates "mocking" rather than "playing." Speiser says it cannot be "mocking," which would require a prepositional prefix (*b-*), but he follows the LXX and Vulgate by adding "with her son Isaac": "When Sarah noticed that the son whom Hagar the Egyptian had borne to

Abraham was playing (with her son Isaac). . . ."[32] Friedman prefers to call it "fooling around."[33]

How one understands what Ishmael is doing relates somewhat to the evaluation of Sarah's subsequent actions. According to Alter, "Some medieval Hebrew exegetes, trying to find a justification for Sarah's harsh response, construe the verb as a reference to homosexual advances."[34] Speiser points out that, according to the text, Ishmael should be at least fifteen years old, and his playing with Isaac should mean no more than an older brother trying to amuse a younger one.[35] He continues: "There is nothing in the text to suggest that he was abusing him, a motive deduced by many troubled readers in their effort to account for Sarah's anger."[36] Cotter understands Sarah's reaction as having nothing to do with the action involved: "When Sarah looks at Ishmael, she does not see the teenaged son of her husband, half-brother to her own son, whose very being is the result of her action . . . ; [she] remembers the humiliation she suffered at Hagar's hands (Gen 16:4) and finds that the time is ripe to wreak her revenge."[37] Von Rad frames it in a similar way by claiming that when Sarah sees the son of Hagar playing with her child, "unpleasant thoughts occur to the calculating woman."[38]

Von Rad's translation and interpretation of Sarah's actions are clearly governed by his understanding of Sarah and her role in the story: "The reader has not expected that the Deity was on Sarah's side, but on Abraham's"—a somewhat common interpretation.[39] Clearly Sarah appears "calculating" if one understands her as a "humiliated" woman whose husband has done nothing but treat her well throughout the story and is only trying to make her happy and protect everyone, as von Rad and others interpret the text. But the best reading of the text shows that Abraham twice gives away his wife to be used sexually by foreign rulers while benefiting financially both times, and that he does not show as much interest in the second son, Isaac, as in the first, Ishmael. Hence, Sarah's calculations and humiliation may not merely be figments of her imagination: her son's position may truly be in jeopardy. Ishmael's close proximity to Isaac, regardless of what is involved in their "play," means that Ishmael has easy access to Isaac. It also shows that Ishmael is treated as a son of Abraham's, not as the son of a slave women. As Turner points out, "Despite Isaac's birth Ishmael is still in the household. Whether Ishmael will be able to maintain his position as heir or not remains to be seen."[40]

One might still argue that Sarah is wrong to want her child to have primacy. Yet, her wish is not merely her own personal preference; the

Deity has promised this as something that will happen (17:16, 21). In fact, according to the rabbis, Sarah is considered one of seven biblical prophetesses, and her prophetic powers are said to have exceeded those of her husband, for she was able to discern the Deity's (Elohim's) will in expelling Hagar and Ishmael, while Abraham resisted.[41] Based on the biblical evidence, from Sarah's perspective, Abraham has handed her off to a foreign ruler immediately following the announcement that she will bear Abraham a child. That would not indicate Abraham's intent to take care of her or her child, if one is conceived in that context. Once again, how one translates and interprets a verse regarding Sarah comes almost as much from one's decision about her role in the text as from grammar and story line.

In 21:10 Sarah emphasizes the role of Ishmael and the matter of inheritance by not using Ishmael's name. She does not say that "Ishmael" should be sent away, but "that slave woman and her son." Some argue that Sarah's annoyance is with Hagar, not Ishmael. On some levels this is true and is borne out by Sarah's constant reference to Hagar. At the same time Sarah raises the question of inheritance, and thus Hagar's status in the family would impact Sarah's understanding of what Ishmael's role in the family is, and what he should and should not inherit, especially vis-à-vis her son, Isaac. In 17:21 the Deity has already made it perfectly clear to Abraham what the role will be between Isaac and Ishmael: "As for Ishmael, I have heeded you. I hereby bless him. . . . But my covenant I will maintain with Isaac, whom Sarah shall bear to you at this season next year" (Gen 17:20–21 NJPS). This is information that Abraham has, based on his conversation with the Deity, though there is no clue in the text that Sarah knows this.

Certain texts from the ancient world, in Genesis, and extrabiblical sources are relevant regarding the status of brothers in a family, especially concerning inheritance. As in Gen 16, there are no law codes from the region of Syro-Palestine that we could consider as contemporary with whatever reasonable date one attributes to Abraham and company. We just do not know enough about the laws or customs they may have brought with them, and the relevance of those laws in their new context. These codes do inform us that others in the ancient world faced the issues that the characters in the patriarchal stories met. The codes also suggest some ways in which other groups attempted to deal with these issues.

The Laws of Lipit Ishtar are from the ancient southern Mesopotamian city of Isin in approximately 1930 B.C.E.[42] The regulations in the composition are concerned primarily with the free person, including the child, in adoption and inheritance.[43] Three in particular deal directly with the relationship between the children of different women related to a man and the status of their children and inheritance.

> If the second wife whom he marries bears him a child, the dowry which she brought from her paternal home shall belong only to her children: the children of the first-ranking wife and the children of the second wife shall divide the property of their father equally. (Lipit Ishtar 24)[44]

> If a man marries a wife and she bears him a child and the child lives and a slave woman also bears a child to her master, the father shall free the slave woman and her children; the children of the slave woman will not divide the estate with the other children of the master. (Lipit Ishtar 25)[45]

> If his first-ranking wife dies and after his wife's death he marries the slave woman (who had borne him children), the child of his first-ranking wife shall be his (primary) heir; the child whom the slave woman bore to her master is considered equal to a native free-born son, and they shall make good his (share of the) estate. (Lipit Ishtar 26)[46]

Thus, according to the Laws of Lipit Istar the status of the second wife determines whether or not the second woman's child inherits. As we saw in Gen 16, the status of Hagar is not clear. It appears that she is originally promoted to the rank of a wife (16:3) and later demoted to a slave (16:6), and thus Sarah has little to fear.

The code of Hammurabi also has something to say on this issue that would concern Sarah more:[47]

> If a man's first-ranking wife bears him children and his slave woman bears him children and the father during his lifetime then declares to (or concerning) the children whom the slave woman bore to him, "my children," and he reckons them with the children of the first-ranking wife-after the father goes to his fate, the children of the first-ranking wife and the children of the slave woman shall equally divide the property of the paternal estate, the preferred heir is a son of the first-ranking wife, he shall select and take a share first. (Code of Hammurabi 170)[48]

According to this rule, if Abraham recognizes the son as his child at some point in his lifetime, then upon his death Ishmael would inherit with Isaac. Still according to this law, Isaac would be the primary heir, but Sarah's statement shows that she views Hagar as a slave and does not want her son inheriting anything. Again, neither the examples of Lipit Ishtar nor Hammurabi prove anything concerning our particular case, but they do provide some background as to what may be issues underlying Sarah's actions.

Some texts in Genesis are also relevant for the discussion, and these concern the relationships among the children of Leah, Rachel, Zilpah, and Bilhah. These passages are especially important since both Zilpah and Bilhah carry the designation of *shifchah*, appear to have some status changes, and have children who inherit. The reference to Hagar's slave status in 21:10 is not the same as in 16:1, where Hagar is first introduced as a *shifchah* belonging to Sarah. Here in 21:10 Hagar is an *'amah*. Though the difference between the two is not always clear, men tend to give *shifchot* (plural) directly to women.

Thus, Laban, father of Leah and Rachel, gives Zilpah directly to Leah as a *shifchah* (29:24), and likewise Bilhah to Rachel (29:29). Already in 30:3 Bilhah is described as an *'amah*, then in 30:4 Bilhah is named a *shifchah* again, precisely when Rachel gives her to Jacob as a wife (*'ishah*), just as Sarah gives Hagar to Abram (16:3). In 30:7 Bilhah again is a *shifchah*, though she seems engaged in activity similar to when she receives the designation "wife" (bearing a child to Jacob). In 30:9 Zilpah is Leah's *shifchah* when Leah gives her to Jacob like a wife, just as Bilhah is given to Jacob and Hagar to Abraham. In 30:10 Bilhah bears a child while retaining the title *shifchah*. Both Bilhah and Zilpah retain the title of *shifchah* when Jacob places them and their children first (the most dangerous place) in the meeting between Esau and Jacob (33:2). The situation becomes slightly more complicated with Bilhah when Reuben, the son of Leah, lies with Bilhah immediately following the death of Rachel. At that time, the text calls her "his father's *pilegesh*" (35:22), often defined as "concubine," though it is probably more complex than that.[49] Thus, as soon as Rachel dies, Bilhah apparently receives a new status and "ownership" of sorts. Ironically, the next verses summarize Jacob's sons and designate Bilhah and Zilpah each as a *shifchah* of Rachel (35:25) or Leah (35:26). Finally, when Joseph brings bad reports to his father about his brothers, 37:2 refers to Bilhah and Zilpah as "wives/women" of Jacob.

In each case the text treats the children of Bilhah and Zilpah as the sons of Leah and Rachel, though the mothers still retain some maternal identity in their having their own tent as *'amahot* (maids, 31:33). The text names specific mothers and also to whom the mother belongs, Rachel or Leah (as in 35:22–26). Jacob definitely treats the children and their mothers differently throughout the story. For example, when Jacob goes to meet Esau, he endangers the maids (*shifchot*) and their children by putting them first in the caravan; in that incident Jacob also regards Leah and her children as less important than Rachel and her child (33:1–2). Jacob's favoritism toward Joseph and Benjamin among his sons is a major theme of the Joseph story (37:2–50:26). In that case, however, Jacob favors Rachel's biological children above the children of Leah, a proper wife, and of the two maids; hence, a different criterion governs this situation. In the final "blessing" of his children, Jacob discusses each child. Although one may argue about precisely what this list represents, for none of the children is their mother or their mother's status a relevant issue (Gen 49). Jacob may treat his children differently based on who their mother is, but that does not seem to impact inheritance issues.

These examples do not clarify similarities or differences between a *shifchah*, *'amah*, *'ishah*, or *pilegesh*, nor do they settle inheritance rules. What they do display is that later in the book of Genesis, children born of women in a status with similar changing designations as Hagar, inherit equally with the children of the primary wives. One can argue that the situation is different with Leah and Rachel because these primary wives recognize the children of their maids as belonging to them, or that because they are from outside the land of Canaan their practices are different. Without clear articulation in the text as to what is different in Jacob's situation, we do not know if the rules are different for Sarah and Abraham, or if Sarah's actions actually protected her son's inheritance.

What further complicates the situation is that the text never states Abraham's attitude toward Ishmael. The text sometimes refers to Ishmael as Abraham's son (16:15; 17:23, 25–26), but in the story Abraham never utters the word "son" for Ishmael, even when he is pleading on Ishmael's behalf before the Deity (17:18). Abraham appears to be content with Ishmael, arguing for him in front of the Deity (17:18), circumcising him immediately (17:25), and never asking for a son by Sarah nor taking actions encouraging the probability of that event. Nevertheless, the text never says Abraham claims Ishmael as a legitimate heir.

As a result of ambiguity in Abraham's relationship to Ishmael and feelings toward Isaac, the following passage should not be as surprising as they are for some interpreters. According to 21:11, "The thing was very bad in the eyes of Abraham about the situation concerning his son." Most commentators assume that Abraham's feelings show he sympathizes with Ishmael. Jeansonne, however, claims that the matter could refer to Sarah's desire to dismiss Hagar or to the existence of the threat to Isaac.[50] The text does not state which son Abraham is concerned about, or what specific angle of the situation distresses him. According to Turner, Abraham is upset that Ishmael will no longer be his heir.[51] He sees evidence of this in the following verse (21:12), where Elohim reaffirms that Abraham's line will continue through Isaac, but says nothing about inheritance of possessions (cf. 17:16, 19, 22).[52] In light of the whole of 21:12–14, it seems more likely that the son triggering Abraham's distress is Ishmael. Other places the text can be specific: in 22:2 Isaac is the son at risk. Perhaps the ambiguity of 21:11 highlights Abraham's complicated relationship with his sons.

Responding to Abraham's distress, Elohim tells him not to be upset about the boy or his slave woman, to listen to Sarah's voice and do what she says, and to remember that his offspring will continue through Isaac (21:12). Elohim comforts Abraham and again promises also to make a nation of the "son of the slave woman," since Ishmael too is Abraham's seed (offspring, 21:13; cf. 16:10–11; 17:20). Once more, Elohim needs to remind Abraham of the original discussion about Isaac's impending birth, that it is through Sarah's child that the covenant will continue (17:19, 21). The fact that Elohim needs to intercede, remind Abraham of the situation, and reaffirm the promise to take care of Ishmael, shows that there is a substantial reason for Sarah's original fears (21:10). In Jeansonne's view, by telling Abraham to follow Sarah's plan, Elohim confirms that Sarah understands Elohim's plan better than Abraham does.[53] We may find further confirmation of this by asking, if Abraham had trusted the Deity, was planning to continue the covenant through Isaac, and believed that Ishmael would be taken care of, why would he be so distressed? This scene may be the background for the Deity's need to test Abraham in the next chapter (22) since Abraham's actions do not indicate complete acceptance of the plan the Deity lays out in Gen 17.

Elohim also seems to be distancing Ishmael from Abraham by referring to him as the "son of the slave woman," rather than his son. Even when the Deity heeds Abraham and promises to make Ishmael fertile and "a great nation," the Deity does not refer to Ishmael as Abraham's son (Gen 17:20). Abraham may have considered Ishmael his son, though he never states it categorically and neither does the Deity (or Elohim).

According to the Deity (or Elohim), Ishmael belongs to Hagar. When Ishmael is born, the three times that the relationship is stated in two verses refers to Ishmael as the son that Hagar bore Abram, or as Hagar bearing a son to Abram (16:15–16; cf. 16:10, "your offspring"). In Gen 17 Hagar's name does not appear, and only the narrator—not Abraham or the Deity/Elohim—names Ishmael as Abraham's son (17:23, 25; cf. 25:12). In Gen 21 Elohim says that Ishmael is Abraham's "seed/offspring" but does not call him Abraham's son. The difference may be minor; but with 22:2 about to follow, where the Deity names Isaac as Abraham's "only son," the distinction might be relevant.

The Banishment of Ishmael

The text now focuses more on Hagar and Ishmael than on Sarah and her child. While these verses are not about Sarah, they do involve Abraham, or a descendent of his, and therefore need a quick examination, especially since the episode deals with eliminating an heir so that only one remains for the next episode.

Following Elohim's pronouncement that Abraham should heed Sarah and that Ishmael also will become a nation, Abraham takes action. "Abraham arose early in the morning" (21:14). These words tie into the following story of the sacrifice of Isaac: immediately following the Deity's command that Abraham should take Isaac to the place that the Deity will show him, the text also reports, "Abraham arose early in the morning" (22:3). The narrator relates the two episodes, both of which include the possible death of a son of Abraham.

In Ishmael's case, Abraham takes bread and a skin of water and gives them to Hagar, placing them over her shoulder, along with the child (21:14). This part of the verse is somewhat confusing because placing the child on Hagar's back would mean that Ishmael is a small child and could be carried by his mother. According to 16:16 Abraham is eighty-six years old when Ishmael is born, and ninety-nine when he circumcises himself and Ishmael (17:24). Isaac is born approximately one year after the circumcision event (21:2) and is weaned at the beginning of this episode (21:8). This would make Ishmael at least fifteen (maybe sixteen or seventeen) years of age. Speiser summarizes the issue: "The various emendations that have been proposed merely substitute one set of problems for another. An acceptable solution has yet to be discovered."[54] It is possible that, to build up the emotion of the scene, the narrator uses some poetic license to depict Ishmael as younger and more vulnerable, thus making the scene more poignant. The text does not include an age but simply adds a detail that leads the reader's imagination to envision a young child without actually stating so.

He (Abraham) sends "her" away (21:14). The text does not state that he sends away Ishmael, the son, or the child—but the woman. While the child is supposedly on the woman's back, and the reader knows from the scene that Ishmael is with her and therefore he too is sent away, the text does not state that Abraham sends them both. According to the text, Abraham only sends away Hagar.

The text continues that she (Hagar) wanders about in the wilderness of Beer-sheba (21:14). The verb is from the root *tav-ayin-he* (*ta'ah*), "to physically wander."[55] The root means "to err." Hagar is wandering around in the same wilderness in which Abimelech has just given Abraham permission to settle where he pleases (20:15). When Abraham "sends" Hagar, the verb is from *shin-lamed-chet* (*shalach*, 21:14), quite different from Sarah's demand: "Cast out," *gimel-resh-shin* (*geresh*, 21:10). Turner argues that what Abraham does is "softer" than Sarah's command.[56] Might Abraham actually be sending her away from the family but not necessarily banishing Ishmael from Abraham's protection or even the area in which he dwells? Hagar's "wandering" might be purposeful, or perhaps she "errs" in where she is going and becomes lost.

The scene with Hagar and Ishmael is heartrending: a mother, lost in the desert and banished by the man who is supposed to protect her and her child, cannot bear to see her son die (21:15–16). When Hagar bursts into tears, Elohim hears the cry of the boy and calls to Hagar (21:16–17). Even when speaking to Hagar, Elohim's messenger says Elohim has heard the cry of the boy, not Hagar's weeping (21:17). Elohim's messenger then shows her a well of water, thus saving Hagar and her child (21:19). Elohim is with the boy, who grows up to be an expert with the bow and lives in the wilderness of Paran, on the south side of Kadesh-barnea, which is fifty miles south of Beer-sheba (21:20). The text says his mother finds a wife for him from Egypt, thus tying back into her original introduction as an Egyptian slave-girl (21:20–21; 16:1).

This unit has many problems for feminists since Sarah, Abraham, and Elohim treat Hagar so badly. On the most fundamental level, Elohim is true to the Deity's promise to Hagar (16:10) and to Abraham to let Ishmael live by the Deity's favor (17:20). Yet the Deity, or Elohim, never promises to take care of Hagar, only her son. This is a painful reality in the text, and the reference to Hagar finding Ishmael a wife from Egypt might be at the heart of it. Hagar is Egyptian. She is not part of the Israelite clan and never will be. The Egyptians originally take Sarah into a type of captivity and will later enslave the Israelites. The text clearly wants to lift up Hagar's pain and critique the actions of Abraham, Sarah, and possibly even Elohim, using the beauty of the prose and the vivid scene of a mother not wanting to oversee the death of her son. Since Hagar is the major protagonist of the scene, it is clear that the narrator is creating sympathy for Hagar with the reader. The messenger says that Elohim hears only the child and declares to the mother that it is because of the child that Elohim is saving them. This stress in the text makes a clear statement that Elohim is more concerned about Ishmael, though the messenger does speak to Hagar and tell her not to be afraid (21:17). Difficult as this is for a modern audience to handle, it is the reality of the biblical text.

In evaluating Sarah, the impact of this scene is complicated. The narrator is eliciting sympathy for Hagar, and yet Elohim just tells her to brace up ("do not be afraid"), promises again to make a great nation of Ishmael, and shows her water so they can survive. The Deity/Elohim directly responds to Sarah's distress (12:17; 20:6; 21:1, 12), indicating that for reasons never clearly articulated the Deity has chosen Sarah as the mother for beginning fulfillment of the promise (17:21). While modern audiences may sympathize with Hagar, the Deity/Elohim has a clear goal and carries through with it. Juxtaposing the two women and their children highlights the Deity's decision.

What this scene also does is establish a need for the Deity to "test" Abraham (Gen 22). Sarah acts to protect the Deity's wishes. Abraham's actions are more questionable. He does carry through with ejecting Ishmael from his house, but only after Sarah's demand and Elohim's command, and with serious distress over the matter—thus establishing the need to test him. Finally, if Ishmael were still around when the Deity asks Abraham to sacrifice Isaac, in light of Abraham's apparent preference for Ishmael, the request might not have been particularly difficult for Abraham. Only with Ishmael out of the picture is Gen 22 so powerful.

Abraham and Abimelech, Again: Genesis 21:22–34

The Masoretes insert a break following Gen 21:22. This makes narrative sense since the following story involves a discussion of wells and more negotiations between Abimelech and Abraham (21:22–34). This scene involves Abraham and negotiations over wells in the area of Beer-sheba, which seemingly has nothing to do with Ishmael or Isaac. Yet it does establish that for a time Abraham stays in the area of Beer-sheba, in the "land of the Philistines" (21:34). His new residence thus is in the desert region, not far from where the text has just left Hagar and Ishmael (21:21). When the text next focuses on Sarah, following the binding of Isaac, she is not in Beer-sheba but in Hebron, where Abraham has earlier lived with Sarah (13:18; 18:1). Has Abraham moved, and if so, is it to be closer to his son Ishmael? Following the expulsion of Ishmael, the text never records any interaction between Ishmael and Abraham. In connection with Abraham's death, the text simply says that "his sons Isaac and Ishmael" bury him with Sarah in the cave of Machpelah (25:9; cf. 25:12).

The Sacrifice of Isaac: Genesis 22:1–19

The Masoretes begin a new section with the beginning of Gen 22, the section often referred to as the sacrifice or binding of Isaac. Sarah does not appear in this chapter, which highlights her son, his relationship with his father, and the Deity. The text categorically states that Elohim puts Abraham to the test (22:1). As with the Hagar-and-Ishmael situation, the details, while interesting and important, are not as relevant for the concerns here as are some of the major themes and how they impact Isaac and Abraham in their relationship to Sarah. As with the banishment of Ishmael, the beautiful prose enhances the drama of the event as it portrays the scene. The focus of this volume, however, does not allow for a discussion of the narrative's beauty.

This unit begins with a link: "And it happened after these things" (22:1). Precisely what "these things" are is not clear. According to Cotter, the phrase "after these things" places the events chronologically after the events of Gen 21 and also suggests a causal relationship, some hint that these events flow from what has happened.[57] Since the narrative focuses on Isaac, called Abraham's "only son," "these things" likely refer to the birth of Isaac, the banishment of Ishmael so that Abraham is left with only one son of the promise, or even the entire story of Abraham. The link may also influence the reader's understanding of Isaac's age at the time when the events of Gen 22 occur. When the reader last met Isaac, he had just been weaned and might have been about three years old. Here he is old enough to converse with his father, to know that a sacrifice demands an animal, to see that his father does not have one to offer, and to tote wood for the burnt offering (22:6–8). Similar to the case of the banishment of Ishmael (21:9–21), the age indicators are subtle, leaving much to the reader's imagination in terms of weighing what those vague references say about the son's age.

Elohim tells Abraham to take Isaac to a place that Elohim will show him. The way Elohim refers to Isaac is one of the more famous in biblical literature: "Take your son, your only one, the one you love, Isaac," to offer him as a burnt offering (22:2). If Ishmael were still around, the verse would be inaccurate in calling Isaac his only son. As Turner observes, "By the time ch. 22 begins, with the exception of Isaac all other candidates for the position of 'promised son' have been explicitly eliminated by Yahweh (albeit reluctantly by Abraham)."[58] The reality is that since Ishmael is alive, whether Abraham knows it or not, the statement is still not factual. Since the narrator knows that this is not the truth, one therefore may ponder the veracity of the other statement: Is *Isaac* the son whom Abraham loves?

The text connects what is about to happen to Isaac with what has happened to Ishmael, beginning with the same three words: Abraham "rose early the next morning" (21:14; 22:3). On the third day they arrive within sight of the place that Elohim has designated (22:3–4). Abraham separates from the other two young men in their entourage and climbs alone with Isaac (22:5–6). The next verse contains Isaac's first word to Abraham: "Father" (22:7). Abraham's response is the first time in the story that he calls Isaac "my son" (22:8). Isaac asks where the lamb is for the burnt offering, and Abraham assures him that Elohim will provide it (22:7–8).

When the pair arrive at the place identified by Elohim, Abraham lays out the wood, binds his son, lays him on the altar on top of the wood, and is about to slay his son (22:9–10). Abraham's actions are striking to some because he raises no objections. His silence is in sharp contrast to Abraham's request for consideration for Ishmael (17:18); in response, the Deity announces that Abraham's wife Sarah will bear him a son to inherit the promise (17:19, 21). It is in contrast to Abraham's stand for the rights of a theoretical (nonexistent) ten innocent people in Sodom (18:32). It also is in contrast to his deep distress over the banishment of Ishmael (21:11). Here Abraham says nothing and is about to carry out the Deity's request (22:2).

Just as Abraham is about to slay Isaac, a messenger of the Deity calls to him from heaven and tells him not to raise his hand against the boy. Now the Deity knows that Abraham fears Elohim since he would not withhold his son from the Deity (22:2, 11–12). Abraham finds a ram in the thicket and sacrifices it in place of his son (22:13). After Abraham names the site (22:14), the messenger of the Deity speaks again to Abraham. The Deity will bestow blessing upon him and make his descendants as numerous as the stars and the sand; all the nations of the earth will bless themselves by his descendents because he obeyed the Deity's voice (22:15–18).

Critiquing this section is particularly difficult since the prose is so poignant and the scene plays such a prominent role in Judaism. It is the passage read on Rosh Hashanah, and throughout the ages artwork has portrayed it. Though the binding of Isaac appears less frequently in the liturgy of the Catholic Church, it still holds a special place because it is read typologically as the ordeal of Isaac foreshadowing that of Christ.[59] For many, this scene shows the height of Abraham's faith in the Deity. Speiser refers to it as the "profoundest personal experience in all recorded history of the patriarchs."[60] Despite the long and deep traditional interpretation of these verses, we must stress some elements that, when grasped in light of Abraham's actions throughout the book thus far, raise questions about the sincerity and appropriateness of his actions.

First, the Deity testing Abraham means that thus far the Deity is still not convinced of something in Abraham's character. Toward the end of the chapter the messenger states that only "now" the Deity knows that Abraham fears Elohim because he has not withheld his only son from the Deity (22:12). This word implies that prior to this event the Deity is not sure whether Abraham fears the Deity. Ironically, such uncertainty is precisely the reason Abraham uses to justify lying to Abimelech, claiming he did not think there was a fear of the Deity in Gerar (20:11).

There are many reasons why the Deity might not be convinced of Abraham's sincerity: his going to Egypt in the first place (12:11), questioning what the Deity has done for him (15:3), laughing about having a child with Sarah (17:17), and giving away his wife when he is supposed to be having a child with her (20:2), to name only a few. Despite Abraham's record in mistrusting the Deity and the clear statement that the Deity is testing him, many have found difficulty with the test. To a large extent, this difficulty is because readers have viewed Abraham in such a positive light and have excused his actions, even when he does not precisely follow what the Deity commands. Their view is like Speiser's: "Abraham had already proved himself on that count [obedience to the Deity] by heeding the call to leave Mesopotamia and make a fresh start in an unknown land."[61] Trible argues that the test is odd for Abraham since nowhere in the text does he have a problem with attachment.[62] She goes further: "In view of the unique status of Sarah and her exclusive relationship to Isaac, she, not Abraham, ought to have been tested."[63] Yet her argument ignores Abraham's relationship to Ishmael, expressed repeatedly in the text, and offers no reason or evidence that (Sarah's) attachment to a family member is a negative character trait in the book of Genesis.

Why this test? The text states that Abraham passes it, but in light of Gen 21, where he quickly gives away his other son, is this a big deal for him? Since the Deity has already promised all the things listed in 22:17–18, if the Deity allows Abraham to slay his last remaining child, then the Deity either is a liar, creating a serious theological problem for the text, or will have to replace Isaac. On some levels, we can consider Abraham's test almost as much a test of the Deity.

The test also highlights the difference between Sarah's and Abraham's relationships with the Deity. Sarah does not need to be tested. Sarah's dedication, without any direct conversations and promises from the Deity, appears strong throughout the text. Sarah calls on the Deity as judge between herself and Abraham (16:5). She is thankful for the laughter (as a positive feature) that Elohim brings her through Isaac (21:6). Finally, by demanding that Abraham expel Ishmael (21:10), Sarah protects the inheritance in accord with the Deity's statement of what is to happen and the biblical mandate the Deity has given to Abraham (17:19, 21). She does this even though the action itself is difficult for modern readers to handle because of the negative result for Hagar and Ishmael. Elohim confirms the expulsion of Ishmael as the correct move (21:12). Genesis 22 confirms the analysis of this study that the Deity has chosen Sarah, and that Sarah follows the Deity's commands as she understands or overhears them—something that Abraham does not do at all times.

Following the blessing that Abraham receives from the Deity because of his willingness to sacrifice Isaac, the text says that Abraham returns to his servants, they go to Beer-sheba, and Abraham stays in Beer-sheba (22:19). Here the text does not state that Isaac accompanies his father or explain what happens to Isaac or where he goes. Despite an entire chapter devoted to Abraham eventually sending a servant to find a wife for Isaac (Gen 24), the story never lets Isaac and Abraham have another conversation together. This contrasts sharply with the ongoing relationship between Isaac and Sarah. Though the text never depicts them together again, we catch a measure of Isaac's feelings for Sarah when he takes Rebekah as his wife and is "comforted after his mother's death" (24:67).

Despite the modern marking of the text, the Masoretes insert a break in the text following 22:19. The following verses deal with what happens to Abraham's brother Nahor's family in Nahor and helps to set up the next generation. Although the Masoretes insert a more significant break between Gen 22 and 23 than between Gen 21 and 22, for purposes of this volume we will consider 22:20–24 in chapter 6 (below). This study still honors the later break (after 22:24) and discusses reasons for it in chapter 6 (below).

Conclusion

The chapters discussed here contain some of the highlights and low points in the lives of Sarah, Abraham, Isaac, Hagar, and Ishmael. Genesis 20 ties neatly to the previous chapters by emphasizing Abraham's assumptions about how others do or do not fear his Deity. Again, he uses his wife to protect himself, but from what is less clear this time. This case is significantly more egregious than the previous because the Deity has recently informed both Abraham and Sarah that they would have a child together, and it is not clear how giving away Sarah would make the Deity's promise a reality.

Genesis 21 reports the fulfillment of the Deity's promise to both Sarah and Abraham of their child Isaac, who is designated to receive the Deity's promise. Despite numerous chapters preparing for this momentous occasion, the text passes over it quickly, leading directly to the more complicated situation of determining the role that Ishmael will play in the life of the family. Through all of this, the text depicts Sarah as the one following the Deity's commands, despite the severe repercussions of her actions on Hagar and Ishmael.

Sarah's demand for Abraham to banish Ishmael forces Abraham to make difficult decisions. Elohim convinces Abraham to follow Sarah, but his initial wavering may be what finally forces the Deity to test Abraham. Sarah does not need to be tested; her loyalty to the Deity is always clear. Abraham passes the test, though the quickness with which he carries it out leaves his motives open to suspicion—confirmed by the end of the chapter. There the text reports that Abraham returns to Beer-sheba, perhaps without his son (not mentioned, 22:19) and his wife (who is in a different place in 23:2).

Notes

1. L. A. Turner, *Announcement of Plot in Genesis* (JSOTSup 96; Sheffield: JSOT Press, 1990), 82.

2. T. Desmond Alexander, *Abraham in the Negev: A Source-critical Investigation of Genesis 20:1–22:19* (Carlisle, U.K.: Paternoster, 1997), 36.

3. D. Manor, "Kadesh-Barnea," *ABD* 4:1.

4. Ibid.

5. D. R. Seely, "Shur, Wilderness of," *ABD* 5:1230.

6. E. D. Oren, "Gerar," *ABD* 2:989.

7. Ibid., 989–90.

8. E. A. Speiser, *Genesis* (Anchor Bible 1; Garden City, N.Y.: Doubleday, 1985), 148.

9. Ibid., 147.

10. Jeffries M. Hamilton, "Paran," *ABD* 5:162.

11. Ibid.

12. The phrasing here is quite similar to David's request of Bathsheba. He sends and then takes her (2 Sam 11:4).

13. I. N. Rashkow, *The Phallacy of Genesis: A Feminist-Psychoanalytic Approach* (Louisville: Westminster/John Knox, 1993), 47.

14. G. von Rad, *Genesis: A Commentary* (Old Testament Library; Philadelphia: Westminster, 1972), 227.

15. Many have trouble understanding why Abimelech would want an old woman in his "harem." In the Egyptian episode, Abraham, the narrator, and the Egyptian courtiers emphasize Sarai's beauty (12:11, 14, 15). In this episode, there is no reference to Sarah's beauty, indicating that the issue is not necessarily about Sarah or her looks. What may be at issue is power. Abraham appears with many flocks and people (at least according to Gen 13–15) and there is no indication in the text that he has lost wealth or people. Abimelech may be trying to show Abraham who has power. Rape it not about sex but power and this would be a similar example. Throughout history women have been raped and taken into foreign houses as a show of dominance, not infatuation or love. The Hebrew text does not justify or question why this would happen, nor does it raise the problem of her age or looks.

16. Turner, *Announcement of Plot*, 83.

17. Rashkow, *Phallacy in Genesis*, 41.

18. Alexander, *Abraham in the Negev*, 46.

19. In this context the term for the Israelite Deity is "Elohim." One need not assume different sources: Abraham is speaking to someone who probably recognizes a general term for a deity but not Abraham's Deity's name.

20. E.g., W. Brueggemann, *Genesis* (Interpretation; Atlanta: John Knox, 1982), 177; Speiser, *Genesis*, 150–52; von Rad, *Genesis*, 226.

21. S. Pace Jeansonne, *The Women of Genesis: From Sarah to Potiphar's Wife* (Minneapolis: Fortress, 1990), 26.

22. Ibid.

23. The list is quite similar, though not identical, to what Abraham receives in Egypt. Because of Sarai, Abram acquires sheep, oxen, asses, male and female slaves, and camels (12:16). When his wealth is summarized upon leaving Egypt, the text lists Abram's assets as cattle (livestock), silver, and gold (13:2).

24. Speiser, *Genesis*, 150.

25. Ibid., 149.

26. For years scholars have pondered the meaning behind the different terms the Hebrew Bible uses to refer to the Israelite deity. One common explanation is that different names reveal different "authors" for the text. There are many scholarly discussions about why and how this approach does and does not work. Since the present author is treating the text as a unified whole, and the presentation of Sarah and Abraham is consistent throughout textual blocks that use YHWH and Elohim, we will refer to the name of the Deity as the Hebrew Bible uses it in the discussions but consider the terms interchangeable.

27. Jeansonne, *Women of Genesis*, 27

28. Ibid.

29. Von Rad, *Genesis*, 231.

30. R. Alter, *Genesis: Translation and Commentary* (New York: Norton, 1996), 97.

31. Von Rad, *Genesis*, 232.

32. Speiser, *Genesis*, 155.

33. R. E. Friedman, *Commentary on the Torah: With a New English Translation and the Hebrew Text* (San Francisco: HarperSanFrancisco, 2001), 71.

34. Alter, *Genesis*, 98.

35. Speiser, *Genesis*, 155.

36. Ibid.

37. D. W. Cotter, *Genesis* (Berit Olam; Collegeville: Liturgical Press, 2003), 141.

38. Von Rad, *Genesis*, 232.

39. Ibid., 233.

40. Turner, *Announcement of Plot*, 85.

41. K. Pfisterer Darr, "More Than the Stars of the Heavens: Critical, Rabbinical, and Feminist Perspectives on Sarah," in *Far More Precious Than Jewels: Perspectives on Biblical Women* (Gender and the Biblical Tradition; Louisville: Westminster/John Knox Press, 1991), 117.

42. M. Roth, *Law Collections from Mesopotamia and Asia Minor* (SBL Writings from the Ancient World; Atlanta: Scholars Press, 1995), 23.

43. Ibid., 24.

44. Ibid., loc. cit., trans. M. Roth.

45. Ibid.

46. Ibid.

47. For discussion of the law code of Hammurabi, see chapter 3 (above), on Gen 16.

48. Roth, *Law Collections*, loc. cit., trans. M. Roth.

49. For a discussion of the problems of the term "concubine," see T. Schneider, *Judges* (Berit Olam; Collegeville: Liturgical Press, 2000).

50. Jeansonne, *Women in Genesis*, 28.

51. Turner, *Announcement of Plot*, 86.

52. Ibid.

53. Jeansonne, *Women in Genesis*, 28.

54. Speiser, *Genesis*, 155.

55. BDB, 1073

56. Turner, *Announcement of Plot*, 87.

57. Cotter, *Genesis*, 152.

58. Turner, *Announcemenet of Plot*, 87.

59. Cotter, *Genesis*, 157.

60. Speiser, *Genesis*, 164.

61. Ibid., 165.

62. P. Trible, "Genesis 22: The Sacrifice of Sarah," in *Women in the Hebrew Bible: A Reader* (ed. A. Bach; New York: Routledge, 1999), 285.

63. Ibid.

CHAPTER 6

Sarah's End:
Genesis 23

Sarah as a living character disappears with the banishment of Ishmael, though she does not die at that point. She is presumably alive when Abraham almost sacrifices their son, Isaac, to the Deity. Many have tried to fill the gaps about Sarah's reaction to Abraham's act of loyalty, but the biblical text is silent on this point. The next time the reader meets Sarah, she is dead. This chapter will examine the paragraph of 22:20–24, between the sacrifice of Isaac and the announcement of Sarah's death, as a major transition to the discussion of the next generation and Isaac's future wife. It will also explore the relationship between this paragraph and the announcement of Sarah's death. Then we will try to ascertain where all the relevant parties are when Sarah dies and how they treat her. Finally, the chapter summarizes Isaac's and Abraham's lives following the death of Sarah.

The Rest of Abraham's Family: Genesis 22:20–24

Immediately following the note that Abraham returns to his servants and journeys back to Beer-sheba, according to the MT, is a small break followed by the announcement that Abraham receives a report about what has happened to his brother Nahor's family. Right after this announcement comes a much larger break, which precedes the death of Sarah. In this context, since I am following the MT, this paragraph should be treated in chapter 5 (above). Yet the paragraph is clearly transitional; it sets up the death of Sarah, the end of focusing on the first patriarch, and the end of this study; hence, I will treat it here.

The section begins with a link: "some time later" (22:20). The wording is identical to the beginning of Gen 22, when the Deity first calls Abraham to sacrifice Isaac. As with 22:1, we wonder: After what? Since the following verses establish the line of Nahor, from whom Isaac's future wife is descended, it may refer to the fact that Abraham almost sacrifices Isaac, whom the Deity's angel saves at the last moment. The text is not clear about such a link, though it seems to be trying to create some relationship between the incidents.

Abraham hears that Milcah too has borne children to his brother Nahor (22:21), and the following verse lists eight sons (22:22). Most scholars assume that the reference that Milcah "too" has borne indicates that "some time later" actually links back to the birth of Isaac, since the implication is that both Milcah and Sarah have borne.[1] No scholars seem particularly interested in the connection of this unit to the near sacrifice of Isaac or to the death of Sarah that is about to come in the text. Yet this reference is significant because the last time the text mentions Milcah is in 11:29, where it introduces Sarai. Genesis 11 juxtaposes the two women and introduces Milcah with a patrimony (daughter of Haran, the father of Milcah and Iscah, 11:29). The next verse mentions Sarai's barren state (11:30). Thus, the reference in 22:20 that Milcah "too" has borne children is slightly ironic: the reader has expected that Milcah would bear and that Sarah would not. Further irony in the statement comes with its timing— not at the birth of Isaac (21:2) or even shortly thereafter, but only after the Deity saves Isaac, recognizing Abraham's willingness or act of faithfulness to sacrifice him.

The text is not bringing Milcah and Nahor back into the story here merely because Sarah is about to die. Their line is also significant because of the connection it will have for Isaac. Genesis 22:22 lists the birth of one of Milcah's children, Bethuel, who in the next verse is identified as the father of Rebekah (22:23). In a few chapters Rebekah will become the bride of forty-year-old Isaac (Gen 24). Although at this point in the narrative the text does not include that information, it does assume that the reader knows the importance of Rebekah because Bethuel is the only son whose children are named. In the story line, the sacrifice of Isaac marks the end of reported direct contact between Abraham and Isaac, and between Abraham and the Deity, and thus on some levels the end of Abraham's generation. What is noteworthy for this study, focusing on Sarah, is the timing of the reference to Milcah bearing and the introduction of Rebekah, who will be the matriarch for the next generation. All this appears in the text not right before the death of Abraham, or even immediately before he sends his servant to Aram-naharaim to find a wife for Isaac, but immediately before the previous matriarch (Sarah) dies. The role of this passage here highlights not only the importance of Rebekah, but also the roles that Rebekah and Sarah fulfill as matriarchs in the story.

With the stress on continuity in the matriarchal line, the text also focuses on Milcah. Abraham hears, "Milcah too has borne children to your brother Nahor" (22:20). After listing her eight sons (22:21) and introducing Rebekah (22:22), the text names Nahor's children by Reumah, Nahor's *pilegesh* ("concubine"? 22:24; see chapter 5, note 49): "And his *pilegesh*, Reumah, also bore. . . ." On one level the construction is similar, but possibly because of Reumah's status as a *pilegesh*, the emphasis is on Nahor because she belongs to him. In the case of Milcah, her name and action appear first, and only later in the sentence does the text mention Nahor. After naming Milcah and Nahor's eight sons, the text summarizes, "These eight Milcah bore to Nahor, the brother of Abraham" (22:23). Hence, twice in the span of four verses the text stresses Milcah's action of bearing children.

The Life of Sarah

The MT includes a large break between 22:24 and Gen 23, with 23:1 beginning a new parashah. The first few words of a parashah or biblical book function as the name for that block of text. In a beautiful ironic twist, "Life of Sarah" is the title for the chapter that recounts the death of Sarah. Despite the name of this chapter, it includes little about Sarah; she dies in the second verse. The focus instead is more on purchasing a burial plot. Although this transaction is not directly about Sarah, it results in the first purchase of land by someone in Abraham's family, and thus becomes a point of continuity. The motivation for the property's purchase and Abraham's reactions to Sarah's death are key factors in evaluating Abraham and Sarah's relationship.

The first verse of Gen 23 measures Sarah's lifetime: a total of 127 years (23:1). The reference is rather striking since Sarah is the only woman for whom the biblical text records the life span. The verse actually names

Sarah two times, though the LXX deletes the second reference. Cotter provides a fairly literal translation, "And Sarah's life was a hundred years and twenty years and seven years: the years of Sarah (Gen 23:1)."[2] He observes how the use of repetition serves to highlight the importance of Sarah and her life, especially since the text uses the same style in the death notices of Abraham and Ishmael (25:7, 17).[3] The grammar of the Hebrew serves to highlight Sarah, the importance of her life, and her role in the story line.

The text claims that Sarah is 127 when she dies. When the Deity announces that she will become the mother of Isaac (17:21), Abraham doubts the news because Sarah is 90 and he 100 years old (17:17). The narrator seems to affirm Abraham's word by reporting that he is 100 at the birth of Isaac (21:5). Thus, according to the limited data in the text, Sarah is 90 or 91 years old at the birth of Isaac. If she is 127 at her death, then Isaac is 36 or 37 when she dies. This interesting chronology implies that Sarah sees her son grow to maturity. The text provides little information about where Isaac and Sarah spend these years. The narrator informs the reader that the binding of Isaac takes place "sometime later" than the events of Gen 21, and that Abraham hears of the birth of Rebekah "sometime later" than the binding of Isaac in Gen 22. The next reference to Isaac's age is that he is 40 years old when he marries Rebekah (25:20). The text states that when Isaac first meets Rebekah, his mother is already dead, though he is still grieving for her (24:67).

The age of Isaac at Sarah's death is relevant because following the rescue of Isaac by the messenger of the Deity, there is no report about where Isaac goes. The text states clearly that Abraham returns to his servants and journeys to Beer-sheba with them (22:19) but is conspicuously silent as to where Isaac goes. The reference to Sarah dying at Kiriath-arba, which the text identifies later as Hebron, further complicates the situation. This possibly means Mamre.[4] The text does not mention any contact between Abraham and Sarah, or even if they were living together, following the binding of Isaac. According to the text's last locale for Abraham before Sarah's death, Abraham is in the northern Negev, at Beer-sheba. In fact, the text is somewhat vague about whether the two were even together when Sarah dies.

The silence of the text as to the whereabouts of the patriarchal family between the end of 22:19 and the death of Sarah has been a source of much discussion. One of the more famous is Rashi's comment: "And the death of Sarah was placed next to the Binding of Isaac, for through the announcement of the Binding, that her son had been prepared for slaughter and had almost been slaughtered, her soul fled from her and she died."[5] The ramifications of Abraham, who expresses little excitement about the original prospect of Isaac, traveling to carry out such an act would have a major impact on Sarah. The text provides room for speculation and does not give details the reader would like to have. The juxtaposition of the near sacrifice and the saving of Isaac, the announcement of the birth of Rebekah, and the death of Sarah while Abraham perhaps is dwelling elsewhere—these scenes are intriguing and beg that we view the incidents together. Unfortunately, the lack of details precludes any conclusions.

The reference to Sarah's death at Kiriath-arba/Hebron is rather surprising. After the couple sets up camp at Mamre (13:18), Abram hears that Lot is kidnapped (14:13), and later the three messengers of the Deity visit the couple (18:1). The place name only appears in the book of Genesis; all instances relate to Abram/Abraham and place the site west of the cave of Machpelah, near (the centuries later) Hebron.[6] The later Israelites know about Kiriath-arba/Hebron, but the references before Sarah's death have them living outside the (later) town and are careful to name the place where the patriarchs are dwelling as Mamre rather than Kiriath-arba/Hebron. Following the destruction of Sodom and Gomorrah (Gen 19), Abraham makes a shift, and all his movements and encounters are in the northern edge of the Negev, and especially at Beersheba (beginning with 20:1). Sarah's return to the area of Hebron is rather striking (cf. 35:27).

The text is a bit oblique about whether the two are together upon her death. Some translations are uncomfortable with the Hebrew: "Abraham came to mourn for Sarah and to cry for her" (23:2), since the implication is that Abraham had to go to her because he was not with her when she dies. Such translations instead treat the verb "to come" as a helping verb, providing a slightly different meaning: "And Abraham proceeded to mourn for Sarah" (NJPS).[7] While not conclusive, the need for Abraham to travel to be with Sarah does not indicate a strong connection between the two, especially post-Gen 22.

In 23:2 Abraham mourns and cries for Sarah. At first glance his actions appear as a sure sign that Abraham greatly misses and mourns his dead wife. The terms in the text provide a different picture. Both terms carry public ritualistic connotations. The second term, *bet-kaf-he* (*bakah*, weep/mourn), is more common and used in more contexts; thus, while carrying a similar connotation as the first, it is a bit more complex. The first term used is more obvious in its public and ritual use. From the root *samelkh-pay-dalet* (*sapad*), it has the base meaning of "wail, lament," especially for the dead, and the lexicon names Gen 23:2 as an example.[8] Other uses of this term in mourning for the dead show that the actions reveal not necessarily personal signs of grief but chiefly public mourning. For example, 1 Sam 25:1 describes all Israel lamenting for Samuel. In the text Samuel has a good reputation. The fact that all Israel carries out the action provides a public demonstration. A more obvious public ritual lamenting is in Jer 16:6: "Great and small alike shall die in this land, they shall not be buried: men shall not lament them. Nor gash and tonsure themselves for them" (NJPS). Speiser uses a Nuzi adoption text to show that "mourning" and "bewailing" are formal rites having no bearing one way or another on the survivor's personal feelings.[9] Abraham clearly goes through the required public rites of mourning, treating her with the public respect due a wife. At the same time, the impact of Sarah's death on him personally is not clarified.

Abraham's next move also carries public acknowledgement of Sarah's role, though again with limited insight into Abraham's personal feelings toward the matter. After mourning his dead, Abraham proceeds to buy land for her burial. He asks the people of the area to let him buy a burial site so he can bury his dead (23:4). Abraham begins by declaring that he is a resident alien (*ger*) among the Hittites (23:4). Commentators observe how the reference reveals that once again Abraham lives among strangers and has no legal rights.[10] From one perspective this continues to be true, but this assessment ignores the role that Abraham plays in ridding the area of foreign rule (14:14–24) and his negotiations in the Negev with Abimelech (20:14–18; 21:22–34). Abraham may officially be a resident alien in the land that the Deity promises him and still be a foreigner. Yet the stories of Abraham's role in the region since his departure from Egypt indicate that he is a savvy player and never fails to come out well in a deal.

The next verses reveal the details of the negotiations between Abraham and the residents of the area, labeled Hittites (23:5–18). Abraham politely asks for land to remove his dead for burial and offers "full price." The Hittites play the same polite role. Much bowing and rhetoric from both sides follow, using ancient Near Eastern legal terminology and practice.[11] Ephron names a price, to which Abraham agrees (23:15–16). What is less clear is who received the best deal. Did Abraham pay a high price to make the point that he is prepared to offer a good price because of the importance of the purchase, or is he trying to be a shrewd businessman? With no land sale contracts from whenever this event supposedly takes place, any response is pure conjecture.

The details of the interaction are fairly intricate, with a fair number of verses on the topic. Yet in most of the interaction, the text seems to lose sight of Sarah's character. This is a business deal, and the depth of the detail seems to indicate an effort to verify and legitimate the purchase. Sarah only returns to the picture once they conclude the business transaction. In fact, even when the text refers to burying Sarah, she is almost an aside in the information: Sarah's burial, name of her spouse (Abraham), the name of the cave (Machpelah), its location (facing Mamre), the later name for that location (Hebron), and the general placement (Canaan). We can recognize this best by examining the number of verses spent on each topic in the chapter. Two verses note the length of Sarah's life and her death, one verse depicts Abraham's acts of mourning, fourteen verses detail the transactions involved in purchasing the plot, one verse summarizes Sarah's burial and placement, and one verse concludes that the field passed from the Hittites to Abraham for a burial site. Clearly, neither Sarah, nor her death, nor the ramifications of her passing are the major focus of the chapter.

Despite Sarah's secondary role in the chapter recording her death, the text presents some fundamental shifts in her relationship with Abraham. In Gen 23 Abraham decides upon a proper and formal burial for Sarah by himself. For the first time neither Sarah nor the Deity must speak or act to protect Sarah from Abraham's actions, especially concerning foreigners. One might argue that Abraham is still concerned about himself since he is purchasing a plot in which he too will one day be interred, but he is prepared, in fact is arranging, to be buried with Sarah. This is the first time in the text thus far that Abraham awards Sarah such honor.

The timing of Abraham's actions is noteworthy. Sarah's death precipitated the action since prior to her death there is no imminent need for a burial plot. Is Sarah's passing what causes Abraham suddenly to understand the importance of Sarah? Again, we remember the juxtaposition of Sarah's death to Abraham's test by the Deity. Is receiving the Deity's approval from passing the test a turning point for Abraham? Another possibility is that the Deity's rescue of Isaac reveals to Abraham that the Deity is serious about making Isaac, the son of Sarah, the heir to the Deity's promise. Of course, a more standard interpretation might argue that the test of sacrificing Isaac is the ultimate point in Abraham's career;

after passing the test, there is no need for Abraham to continue regular communication with the Deity. Whichever is the reality (or some combination of all of them), there is a change in Abraham.

Abraham's Life After Sarah

Following Gen 22 the text does not portray Abraham communicating with the Deity, Isaac (but see 35:27), Sarah, or Ishmael (but see 25:5–6). To a large extent his "career" comes to an end. In the next chapter he sends his servant to find a wife for his son, Isaac, from his kinsfolk, not from the daughters of the Canaanites (24:3–4). However, there is no clue that Abraham ever has a conversation with Rebekah or even knows of her incorporation into the family.

Despite the lack of reported contact between Abraham and Rebekah, Abraham does spend time, effort, and financial resources to find the correct wife for Isaac. This action is another example of how Abraham, either following the binding of Isaac or the death of Sarah, seems to take seriously the notion that Isaac is his heir. In 24:2 Abraham charges his servant with finding for his son a wife who is not from the daughters of the Canaanites, though neither the text nor the narrator explains why. Abraham makes the servant swear that to find the woman he will go back to the land of Abraham's birth (24:4, 7; Ur? Haran? likely Haran since the servant goes to Aram-naharaim). When the servant asks what to do if the woman will not return with him, Abraham stresses that in no way should his son go there (24:6). Abraham then declares with certainty that the Deity will send a messenger and the servant will be successful (24:7, 40). The servant is successful, and things turn out the way Abraham hopes. The text beautifully portrays the servant's own personal scenarios and prayers for guidance, and expressions of faith and worship. Though the text does not depict Abraham and the Deity having direct contact, Abraham does follow the wishes of his Deity, and the Deity helps him and the servant. Have things changed so that now both Abraham and the Deity have similar ideas in mind and no longer need to communicate? Abraham is finally acting according to the Deity's plan and may need no more specific guidance.

After finding a wife for Isaac, Abraham's life shifts from his first family. The text reports that Abraham continues to have a family life, one with another wife, Keturah (25:1), with whom he has six children (25:2). He apparently has concubines as well since the text says that he has children with them (25:6).[12] Yet the text is quite explicit that only Isaac inherits (25:5). Abraham's other children do not inherit. The narrator also explains that Abraham sends them away from his son, Isaac, to the land of the east (25:6). Again, even without the Deity or Sarah reminding Abraham of what to do, he now acts according to the Deity's plan laid out in Gen 17.

The text makes it clear that Abraham has a life far beyond Sarah's death. At his death he is 175 years old, meaning he outlives Sarah by 38 years. If one follows the chronology of the text, Isaac is 60 years old at the birth of his twin sons (25:26), so that Abraham is still alive when they are born. This situation is ironically similar to that of Terah and Abraham, where the text inserts the time of the father's death at a place that is convenient for the story line but conflicts with the chronological data included. The text does not clarify whether this means that, like Abraham, Isaac abandons his father, or whether the numbers are simply an editorial oversight. In all of Abraham's years following the death of Sarah, with the other wife or concubines and children—that section of his life and death warrants a mere ten verses of text (25:1–10). Hence, Abraham's life, either after Moriah (22:2) or following the death of Sarah (23:2) and procuring a wife for Isaac, has no particular meaning for the promise or the Deity. Yet the narrator makes it clear that the Deity blesses Abraham in all things (24:1; cf. Isaac, 25:11) and that he dies content (25:8).

Though Abraham has a later family, when he dies it is his first family that is active in his burial. Upon Abraham's death his sons Isaac and Ishmael bury him in the cave of Machpelah (25:9). This reference is particularly touching in a day when the descendants of Isaac and Ishmael seem to be pitted against each other. Even within the context of the text, the reference is poignant because it indicates that whatever problems existed between the parents, they did not carry over to the sons. When the text mentions the one place where Isaac lives from the time of his marriage, it is precisely at the well that Hagar names after the Deity when she is pregnant with her son, Ishmael, and runs away (16:14; 24:62; 25:11). Those verses give us little to go on, though they suggest possible contacts between Isaac and Ishmael that the text does not verify.

Sarah too reclaims her role as Abraham's wife in his death. When the text reports where Abraham is buried, it says that it is with his wife, Sarah. Despite Abraham's new life following Sarah's death, the new wife (Keturah) does not rank with Sarah; her children do not inherit, and she is not included in the family burial plot. In the narrator's understanding of events, though Abraham has a later wife, she is barely relevant to Abraham's story. In fact, one might argue that reference to the later wife only highlights the importance of Sarah. Abraham's life following the death of Sarah is almost meaningless in the eyes of the narrator and as part of Abraham's legacy.

Sarah in Isaac's Memory

Upon Sarah's death, the text says that Abraham mourns ritually and does not necessarily tell us of any emotional grief. He seems to move on, to have a contented life with little role for Sarah in it following her death. The same is not true for Isaac. While Isaac does not play as major a role in the narrative as either Abraham or Jacob, the text does provide a few glimpses into his interior life. The most relevant for the focus of this study follows Isaac's meeting with Rebekah and his "taking" her as his wife (24:67).

Abraham has his servant swear to find a wife for Isaac from among his own people, in the land of his birth (24:2–4). The servant is successful and brings Rebekah back to Isaac, who at that time is living in Beer-lahai-roi, in the Negev (24:62). The servant tells Isaac what he has done, presumably including his petition to Abraham's Deity where he requests specific signs (24:12–14), which then happen (24:15–27). These happenings prove, at least in the servant's eyes and in response to Abraham's expectations (24:7), that Abraham's Deity makes the events transpire, and the servant blesses and thanks the Deity (24:27). On some levels the episode concludes when Isaac takes Rebekah as his wife (24:67).

The final action is the consummation of the marriage, which completes Abraham's request expressed at the beginning of the chapter. Nevertheless, the text adds a comment prior to Isaac's taking Rebekah and the results of his love for her that throw the entire story back to his relationship with his mother. When Isaac brings Rebekah to the tent, the text adds that it is "the tent of his mother Sarah" (24:66). Little is known about the role of women's tents such as what actions are carried out inside versus outside and who has access to them. The reference to Sarah's name associated in any way with Isaac at such a point in the story is tremendous.[13] Regardless of what happens in a woman's tent, Abraham is the one who commissions the servant to find Rebekah (24:2–4), and Abraham is the one who is still around—though some readers argue that Abraham dies while the servant is completing his mission.[14] Yet is it not

Abraham who is uppermost in Isaac's mind but his mother, Sarah, in whose tent he either dwells or has saved for his future wife.

The text is even more explicit about Isaac's feelings for both his new bride and his mother than anything ever revealed about Abraham. The text claims, "Isaac loved her [Rebekah]," and "Isaac was comforted after his mother." The precise meaning of "after his mother" is somewhat open to interpretation. Friedman translates "consoled after his mother," which works well since part of the problem is how to translate "after his mother,"[15] which seems to beg for completion. Speiser associates the "after" with Akkadian *arki*, which carries the connotation of "after the death of": "comforted after the death of his mother."[16] Regardless of the precise meaning, the thrust of the verse is that Isaac misses his mother as long as three or four years after her death. He mourns his mother, and with Rebekah he finds comfort. Sarah expresses joy at the birth of Isaac (21:6) and clearly seeks to protect Isaac and his inheritance (21:10). Here the text assures readers of Isaac's love for his mother in return (24:67).

Conclusion

This chapter begins with the end of Gen 22 because of its transitional role in linking the end of Sarah's life, and to a large extent the Abraham cycle, with the beginning of the text's focus on Isaac and Rebekah (22:20–24). The reference to the future matriarch's family neatly rounds out the focus on Sarah's life, emphasizing how far she has come since 11:29, where she is childless and barren, to that present, where she has her much desired son.

Though Gen 23 is named "The Life of Sarah" and deals with her death, the chapter contains little information about her or her relationship with Abraham or Isaac. Ironically, it is in asides in the later chapters where the impact of Sarah and her life are revealed. Her husband Abraham, even though he finds a new wife and has children following her death, recognizes her importance in the promise and is buried with her. Since there is no reference to the new wives being in the cave of Machpelah, it seems he keeps the new wife out of the burial plot. Isaac simply mourns his mother.

Either Sarah's death, the saving of Isaac from imminent sacrifice by the Deity, or notification that Abraham passes the Deity's test, seems to change Abraham. While he moves on with his life following Sarah's passing, he honors her in her death in a way that he never does when she is alive. He does this by looking out for her son, Isaac, and recognizing her importance by buying the burial plot for her that is then used for the primary matriarchs and the patriarchs through the demise of Jacob.[17] Abraham also looks out for her son, Isaac, by obtaining a wife for him and giving him the inheritance, "all he had" (24:36; 25:5). The Deity has blessed Abraham in all things (24:1), and now Isaac also inherits Elohim's blessing (25:11). Thus, the story moves on to the next generation of the covenant people. Sarah's role as generating the covenant people is celebrated in Isaiah 51:2, where she is referenced as the one "who brought you forth" (NJPS).

Notes

1. E. A. Speiser, *Genesis* (Anchor Bible 1; Garden City, N.Y.: Doubleday, 1985), 163; C. Westermann, *Genesis: A Practical Commentary in Text and Interpretation* (trans. D. Green; Grand Rapids: Eerdmans, 1987), 163.

2. D. W. Cotter, *Genesis* (Berit Olam; Collegeville: Liturgical Press, 2003), 162.

3. Ibid.

4. The text clearly identifies Kiriath-arba and Hebron as the same city (Gen 23:2, Josh 14:15, Judg 1:10). The relationship of Mamre to Kiriath-arba/Hebron is less clear. The text only refers to Mamre in Genesis and all the references are associated with Abram/Abraham. See J. M. Hamilton, "Kiriath-arba," *ABD* 4:84 and Y. L. Arbeitman, "Mamre," *ABD* 4:492–93

5. Cotter, *Genesis*, 161.

6. Y. L. Arbeitman, "Mamre," 4:492–93.

7. Speiser, *Genesis*, 168.

8. BDB, 704.

9. Speiser, *Genesis*, 169.

10. Ibid., 172; Cotter, *Genesis*, 162–63.

11. Cotter, *Genesis*, 162

12. The term used for these women is the plural of the *pilegesh*.

13. For a discussion of women's tents, see T. Schneider, *Judges* (Berit Olam; Collegeville: Liturgical Press, 2000).

14. For example, see Speiser, *Genesis*, 183, on the symbolism of placing the hand on the adjurer's thighs (Gen 24:2). The text duplicates this only in 47:29, on Jacob's deathbed. Combining this setting with the fact that the servant refers to Isaac as "my master" upon return from his mission means that Abraham actually died while the servant was on his mission. Hence, the reason there is no contact between Rebekah and Abraham is that Abraham dies before any contact could take place—in Speiser's interpretation.

15. Richard Elliott Friedman, *Commentary on the Torah: With a New English Translation and the Hebrew Text* (San Francisco: HarperSanFrancisco, 2001), 85.

16. Speiser, *Genesis*, 182. For the definition of *arki* with the meaning of "after the death of PN," see A. Leo Oppenheim, "Arki," *CAD*, vol. 1: *A, Part 2*: 278.

17. The exception to this is Rachel, who dies in childbirth and is buried along the journey, at Ephrath (later called Bethlehem, 35:18–19). Also note that though the children of Bilhah and Zilpah inherit, they are not interred in the burial cave.

Conclusions

This study treats the character of Sarah from a slightly different perspective than those done previously. In this chapter I summarize the results and conclusions of my analysis. Some may wonder, If the present author's thesis is correct, how could scholars have missed these points for so long? To answer that question, this chapter will briefly consider some presuppositions of previous generations of scholars. The appendix will then consider how some of these presuppositions raised in this conclusion entered biblical interpretation by examining a text that has had a huge impact on the interpretation of the Hebrew Bible, the New Testament. The role of Sarah—and as a result Hagar—and Abraham in the New Testament will serve as an example to consider the role that document may have played in the interpretation of the first patriarchal family through the ages. I use the New Testament because it is a fairly ancient document and has had a significant impact on such a large number of people for so long. This study will consider what this new image of Sarah—and as a result Abraham, Hagar, Isaac, and Ishmael—means for understanding the book of Genesis and the Bible as a whole.

Who Are These People?

Using the grammar, syntax, vocabulary, and the Masoretic blocking of the MT of Genesis, this study has introduced rather different images of some of the major characters in the book. The initial starting position is that the MT, including the consonants and also the blocking of the text, is the starting place. So is the concept that, regardless of the history of development of the text, the narrative is a unified document. Most of the translations and interpretations of the material in this study stem from a close reading of the text and an attempt to make sense of the text before assigning to it any type of interpretation, theological or otherwise.

Such an approach first raises the role of the tower of Babel incident and Genesis 11 in general. Despite the traditional separation of Genesis 1–11 from the rest of the book, the connections between Gen 11–12 are strong and intentional. In particular, the tower of Babel incident is neatly tied to both the genealogy of Terah (and therefore Abram) and, because of the language employed, Gen 12. The connection with Gen 12 sets the tone, to some extent, for the Deity's attitude toward Abram/Abraham in the rest of the book. Abraham may not be so innately wonderful that the Deity chooses him; instead, the Deity's choice is to show, intentionally, that the Deity is the one who makes a name great. In other words, the Deity can make even Abram look good.

The genealogy of Terah introduces characters who will occupy the reader's attention for the rest of the book, not only Abram and Sarai but also the rest of Abram's brothers and their children, especially Abram's brother Nahor, whose daughter Rebekah becomes an important matriarch. The emphasis on the genealogy and the introduction of characters who become important later prove that the Deity, or the author/narrator/editor, is not intending a clean break with everything that happens before Abram's trek to Canaan: continuity with family is essential. The importance of marrying the correct person, an element emphasized more in the later narrative with Abram's descendants, is introduced already in Gen 11 through the genealogy, though its role may not be not readily apparent when originally stated.

This study's translation and interpretation of Gen 12:1–9 invites the reader to question what is really asked of Abram and whether he follows the Deity's instructions as closely as is usually assumed. It also places more emphasis on precisely what the Deity promises Abram that forces the reader to consider later events in light of the Deity's promise, events such as Hagar's "humbling" of Sarai (Gen 16) and Abram's letting Lot choose in which land to settle (Gen 13).

By considering Gen 12:10–13 as one unit of text, and treating together the events in Egypt and Abram's later interaction with Lot—this strategy forces the reader to reevaluate and identify the important elements that the text lifts up in each of these chapters. Questioning Abram from the beginning places his actions in Gen 12:10–20 in a less favorable light and establishes the basis from which Sarai functions throughout the rest of the narrative. Again, by tying Gen 12 to what follows, especially in comparison with the way that Abram treats Lot, provides the reader with a slightly different vantage point from which to consider and treat Sarai's later actions.

Traditionally, interpreters do not consider Gen 16 in relation to Gen 14 and 15. As this study has shown, in these chapters Abram goes through a major transformation in terms of his role in the region, a change that seems to manifest itself even in his relationship with his Deity. This study then examines Sarai's actions in Gen 16 in light of the new Abram, the result of Gen 14–15. We combine Sarai's past experience in Egypt with an understanding of the roles of slaves responsible to their owners, as expressed in the law codes of the ancient Near East, and the Deity's promise in Gen 12:2. As a result, Sarai's actions in Gen 16 make much more sense and fit their context better than as traditionally presented.

After the chaos of Gen 16, or possibly as a result of the major characters' actions in that chapter, the Deity becomes much more specific in Gen 17 as to what the promise is and who will receive it. Genesis 17 presents transformations significant for Abraham, Sarah, and their descendants: here for the first time the Deity becomes specific about who will carry on the promise. Chapter 17 ends with the physical manifestation of Abraham's commitment to the Deity, though Abraham may be focusing too much on Ishmael.

My translation of 18:15 demands a reanalysis of 18:1–15. Traditionally, readers have interpreted Sarah's actions in the rest of the chapter through the lens of her reprimand from the Deity. Once we understand that the Deity does not reprimand Sarah, then all of her actions prior to that verse take on a new tone. The theme of 18:1–15, and even of Gen 19, shift significantly when one acknowledges the Masoretic treatment of Gen 18 as one unified chapter. In their sectioning of the text, the focus is not on Sodom but more obviously on whom Abraham protects and whom he does not. This analysis shows clearly that, once again, Abraham does not protect his wife; instead, he protects a city that does not fear the Deity.

The next chapter, Gen 20, follows that theme by telling how Abraham suspects the king of Gerar of what the people of Sodom are actually doing. He uses this as an excuse to abandon his wife a second time. This analysis highlights how problematic Abraham's action is, especially in light of what he knows from having done it once before (12:10–20) combined with the Deity's recent promise of an heir through Sarah. This then ties directly to the events of Gen 21, where the birth of Isaac places Abraham in a bind, forcing him to choose between his two sons. Despite Abraham's apparent favoritism for Ishmael, Sarah's wishes prevail, backed up by the influence of the Deity. The study treats the banishment of Ishmael in light of the Deity's promise in Gen 17, thus revealing that the blame for the events may be more on Abraham. He does little or nothing to indicate to Sarah or the Deity that he is prepared to carry through, to make the Deity's promise a reality. The result of Abraham's unclear intentions seems to be the basis of the Deity's need to test Abraham in Gen 22, where only Abraham is tested.

This study ends with the death of Sarah, only announced after the narrative ties her again to Milcah and others of Abraham's family, first introduced in Gen 11. The text treats her death primarily as a bracket for an extended account of Abraham buying land for her burial plot. Despite the lack of any personal grief revealed in the text, Abraham's following actions indicate that after the binding of Isaac, he may finally have changed in his attitude to both Sarah and Isaac. All his subsequent actions are in line with the Deity's pronouncement in Gen 17. Although the text does not portray direct conversation between the Deity and Abraham following the near sacrifice of Isaac and the death of Sarah, his actions do secure Sarah's memory and Isaac's future.

Through all these events, this study clarifies Sarah's role. Her husband, Abraham, treats her poorly. Despite no report of direct contact between Sarah and the Deity, she stays in line with the Deity's demands and promises, going to extremes to help make those promises a reality. The Deity recognizes Sarah's efforts and in return saves and protects her continually from Abraham's actions. Eventually the Deity presents her with the son who provides her the status of matriarch. Sarah's son, Isaac, clearly appreciates his mother's role and, even several years after her death, still mourns her, until his wife, Rebekah, comforts him.

Why So Wrong?

One legitimate question resulting from this analysis is that, if the text is so clear about the roles of Sarah and Abraham, why have scholars been so wrong all these years? The answer to that question could take volumes of books to answer. To a large extent readers have tied their interpretations to the role that these characters play in the traditions of the rabbis and the New Testament, and the theology that flows from both groups. Most of the rabbis and Christian theologians responsible for interpreting the text have adopted the controlling assumption that the patriarchs are positive role models and must be innately good; otherwise the Deity would not have picked them as *the* patriarchs. Let me again cite Barry Eichler:

> Within an interpretive community that views the patriarchs as paragons of virtue and their life-narratives as edifying instructions to future generations such ambiguity cannot be tolerated. Jewish and Christian exegetes throughout the ages have focused most of their interpretive efforts on dispelling these ambiguities in their realistic reading of the text.[1]

Since such seems to be the case—which most scholars recognize on some levels—then readers have not earlier noticed many interpretations of the various characters as I present them in this volume. This has happened not because the text does not present the characters as such, but because earlier generations of exegetes let previously held assumptions restrict them from such interpretations. Interpretations of Sarah in the New Testament are part of this puzzle.[2]

Where Do We Go from Here?

Theology has guided many commentaries even when the authors and scholars of the volumes thought they were dealing with grammar and syntax. In a number of fields through the last century and into this one, scholars have been discussing how and whether interpreters should separate themselves from their own previously held beliefs and opinions. This is difficult to accomplish. What this study has attempted to do is take one particular perspective, clearly a feminist one, and see what applying that perspective throughout the text reveals. By grounding the bulk of the data used to define the character of Sarah in points of grammar, syntax, and blocking of MT, one goal is to highlight how biases of previous scholars are at least as problematic as anything carried out or proposed in this volume.

The present study also focuses more attention than most essays of this sort on the actions of the male characters surrounding Sarah. Rather than excluding the connecting material, I have incorporated it into the evaluation because the other characters in the text change under the influence of their experiences. From examining the connecting material, a quite different characterization of Sarah emerges than scholars usually present. Another result of focusing on Sarah and the development of the characters around her is that we can view the surrounding characters from a different vantage point. Thus, Sarah becomes not just the wife of the patriarch; instead, the Deity chooses Sarah as surely as Abraham, especially in terms of the continuation of the promise. The question of why the Deity tests Abraham rather than Sarah is no longer difficult to answer.

This different image of Sarah and Abraham, as well as of the rest of their family, makes a significant impact on our understanding of the book of Genesis. We now are able to see the role of the Israelite Deity and the Deity's decision to choose Abraham and his family through Isaac as related more closely to the so-called primeval history. Yet there are still many issues in Genesis that do not make complete sense, despite the vast amount of research on so many of the possible topics. For example, why does the text name some women and not others? Why and how is the Tamar story imbedded, apparently, in the middle of the Joseph story (Gen 38)? The next logical step is a study such as this, focusing on the women in the narrative of Genesis and examining how the actions of their men impact them, the other men, and the Deity.

Various commentaries are on the market, all taking a slightly different approach to the text, whether form-critical or literary or whatever. Feminist approaches to the biblical text are still somewhat in their infancy. There have been great strides in the last thirty years or so, but there is still much to do. One problem is that, to a large extent, the studies on women in the biblical text are focused studies, such as this, examining one particular character or a trend that applies primarily to the female characters. What would a commentary series examining each book individually from a feminist perspective offer not only for feminist scholarship, but also for our understanding of the biblical text in general?

Despite thousands of years of scholarship on the Hebrew Bible, the text still fascinates and confounds most readers. The text provides enough information about the characters and their situations to draw the reader into the narrative, and yet provides enough gaps in the stories to leave the text open for numerous possibilities and interpretations. This volume is one more offering in the long tradition of engaging the text seriously, a task that hopefully will continue for the next few thousand years.

Notes

1. Barry Eichler, "On Reading Genesis 12:10–20," in *Tehillah le-Moshe: Biblical and Judaic Studies in Honor of Moshe Greenberg* (eds. Mordechai Cogan, Barry L. Eichler and Jeffrey H. Tigay; Winona Lake: Eisenbrauns, 1997), 28.

2. See "Appendix: The New Testament," below.

Appendix:
The New Testament

The New Testament supplies several proof texts that the Christian community has used to shape its understanding of Sarah and her character. The bulk of modern scholars commenting on the book of Genesis are Christian, and as a result they also make a short examination of Sarah's presentation in the New Testament. There are few references, and their preliminary emphases fairly easy to present. Other influences on exegetes may be just as powerful, but the New Testament references are the easiest with which to make the point.

I am not a specialist in the New Testament, early Christianity, or Christian theology. Yet my comments here are fairly basic, and I have drawn them from references in many of the commentaries cited and consulted for this volume. They are preliminary and take the New Testament, to a certain extent, at face value. Still, they are references to Sarah, and by extension to Abraham and Hagar, in a text that many regard as biblical. Hence, these few verses clearly influence how readers, scholars, and theologians understand these characters.

The New Testament treatment of Sarah particularly shows why she appears so differently in traditional interpretations than in this study. In Romans 4:19 Paul mentions Sarah only insofar as she is barren. He does not take her barren state to say anything about her but emphasizes the faithfulness of Abraham. Sarah is barren, and so Abraham must be faithful to believe that he can have a child with her. The New Testament states this as fact, and to some extent, if one is buying into the New Testament as the final word, than no other interpretation of Abraham's actions in the Hebrew Bible is possible. Hebrews 11:11 treats Abraham (and Sarah?) as believing that he (being old) and his wife (being barren) can still have the child of promise. Thus, they exemplify faith in God, who is faithful.

Sarah's role as a holy woman becomes problematic, certainly for feminists, because of her role in 1 Peter 3:6. The text uses Sarah as an example of holy women who trust in God by subjecting themselves to their husbands. Proof of this here is the claim that Sarah obeys Abraham, calling him "lord."[1] The reference uses Gen 18:12 as its proof text, where Sarah first learns that she is going to have a child. She refers to her husband as 'adonai, "my lord" or "my husband." The irony is that Genesis itself has this verse in the context of Sarah's exclaiming, "Shall I have joy [possibly sexual] with my husband so old?" Sarah's reference in the Hebrew Bible questions, on some levels, not that the Deity will allow her a child at such an old age, but that her husband will be able to adequately perform his physical fathering role. One could read her statement as questioning Abraham's virility, and yet the New Testament sanitizes the reference and turns it into a sign of submission by Sarah. Again, because the New Testament states this categorically, it seems to deny any other interpretation of the verse.

The last New Testament reference is fraught with difficulties because of its anti-Semitic potential.[2] Galatians 4:21–31 seems to address the Jews. Along the way it discusses the relationship between Sarah and Hagar and in 4:30 quotes from the Hebrew Bible (Gen 21:10) Sarah's declaration to Abraham: "The son of that slave woman shall not inherit with my son." What the New Testament then does is associate Hagar with slaves, and Sarah with free people. The result is to identify the free with those in the present audience who rely on God's promise, and Hagar and her children with those enslaved to the law (likely Judaizers within the church). Paul calls this an allegory for his present charges, and hence it is a use of symbolism from Genesis rather than a thoroughgoing exegesis of the relevant passages there.

The Galatians passage is a touchy text, whose ramifications are significant. Especially in the United States, where slavery has made its unique stamp, a biblical justification for one group being free while another is enslaved, carries with it painful racial connotations. Regardless of what the Hebrew Bible's approach to slavery is, and what being a free person versus a slave may mean in this text, something strange can happen with interpretation here. People tend to read Sarah's actions in Gen 21 through the treatment of the verse in Galatians, and then filter all that through the United States lens of slavery. This interpretive procedure casts Sarah in an extremely bad light of driving out and disinheriting the slave (Gal 4:30), whether she deserves that reputation or not.

The history of biblical scholarship is a topic in its own right. It deserves more attention than this brief summary of one ancient source and a few ideas about the attitudes of previous generations of scholarship. Since the history of scholarship is not the focus of this volume, I will leave the topic for others to examine.

Notes

1. Note how this counters what Elohim tells Abraham to do in 21:12, where Elohim tells Abraham to listen to Sarah's voice.

2. Gale A. Yee, "Sarah," *ABD* 5:982.

Bibliography

ABD. *See* Freedman, D. N., ed.

Alexander, T. Desmond. *Abraham in the Negev: A Source-critical Investigation of Genesis 20:1–22:19*. Carlisle, U.K.: Paternoster, 1997.

Alter, Robert. *Genesis: Translation and Commentary*. New York: Norton, 1996.

Arbeitman, Yoel L. "Mamre." *ABD* 4:492–93.

Astour, Michael C. "Ellasar." *ABD* 2:476–77.

————. "Goiim." *ABD* 2:1057.

BDB. *See* Brown

Bottéro, Jean. "The 'Code of Hammurabi.'" Pages 156–84 in *Mesopotamia: Writing, Reasoning and the Gods*. Chicago: University of Chicago Press, 1992.

Brown, F., S. R. Driver, and C. A. Briggs. *A Hebrew and English Lexicon of the Old Testament: With an Appendix Containing the Biblical Aramaic*. Oxford: Clarendon, 1907.

Brueggemann, Walter. *Genesis*. Interpretation: A Bible Commentary for Teaching and Preaching. Atlanta: John Knox, 1982.

CAD. *See* Roth, Martha T.

Cotter, David W. *Genesis*. Berit Olam. Collegeville: Liturgical Press, 2003.

Dandamayev, Muhammad A. "Slavery (ANE)." *ABD* 6:58–62.

Darr, Katheryn Pfisterer. "More Than the Stars of the Heavens: Critical,

Rabbinical, and Feminist Perspectives on Sarah." Pages 85–131 in *Far More Precious Than Jewels: Perspectives on Biblical Women*. Gender and the Biblical Tradition. Louisville: Westminster/John Knox Press, 1991.

Davila, James A. "Shinar." *ABD* 5:1220.

Diakonoff, I. M. "Slave-Labour vs. Non-Slave Labour: The Problem of Definition." Pages 1–3 in *Labor in the Ancient Near East*. Edited by M. A. Powell. Copenhagen: Akademisk Forlag, 1987.

Eichler, Barry. "On Reading Genesis 12:10–20." Pages 23–38 in *Tehillah le-Moshe: Biblical and Judaic Studies in Honor of Moshe Greenberg*. Edited by Mordechai Cogan, Barry L. Eichler, and Jeffrey H. Tigay. Winona Lake: Eisenbrauns, 1997.

Exum, J. Cheryl. "Who's Afraid of 'The Endangered Ancestress'?" Pages 141–56 in *Women in the Hebrew Bible: A Reader*. Edited by A. Bach. New York: Routledge, 1999.

Fewell, Dana, and David Gunn. *Gender Power and Promise: The Subject of the Bible's First Story*. Nashville: Abingdon, 1999.

Freedman, D. N., ed. *Anchor Bible Dictionary*. 6 vols. New York: Doubleday, 1992.

Friedman, Richard Elliot. *Commentary on the Torah: With a New English Translation and the Hebrew Text*. San Francisco: HarperSan Francisco, 2001.

Fuchs, Esther. "The Literary Characterization of Mothers and Sexual Politics in the Hebrew Bible." Pages 117–36 in *Feminist Perspectives on Biblical Scholarship*. Edited by A. Yarbro Collins. Atlanta: Scholars Press, 1985.

Goldingay, John. "The Patriarchs in Scripture and History." Pages 1–35 in *Essays on Patriarchal Narratives*. Edited by A. R. Millard and D. J. Wiseman. Leicester: Inter-Varsity Press, 1980.

Greengus, Samuel. "Legal and Social Institutions of Ancient Mesopotamia." Pages 469–84 in vol. 3 of *Civilizations of the Ancient Near East*. Edited by Jack Sasson. New York: Charles Scribners Sons, 1995.

Greifenhagen, F. V. *Egypt on the Pentateuch's Ideological Map: Constructing Biblical Israel's Identity*. JSOTSup 361. London: Sheffield Academic Press, 2002.

Hall, Robert. "Circumcision." *ABD* 1:1025–31.

Hamilton, Jeffries M. *ABD* 5:162.

Heard, R. Christopher. *Dynamics of Diselection: Ambiguity in Genesis 12–36 and Ethnic Boundaries in Post-Exilic Judah*. Atlanta: Society of Biblical Literature, 2001.

Hess, Richard S. "Chaldea." *ABD* 1:886–87.

Jeansonne, Sharon Pace. *The Women of Genesis: From Sarah to Potiphar's Wife*. Minneapolis: Fortress, 1990.

Manor, Dale. "Kadesh-Barnea." *ABD* 4:1–3.

Millard, A. R. "Abraham." *ABD* 1:35–41.

Moorey, P. R. S. *Ur "Of the Chaldees": A Revised and Updated Edition of Sir Leonard Woo Leicester lley's Excavations at Ur.* Ithaca: Cornell University Press, 1982.

Noth, Martin. *A History of Pentateuchal Traditions*. Englewood Cliffs, N.J.: Prentice-Hall, 1972.

Oren, Eliezer. "Gerar." *ABD* 2:989.

Pollack, Susan. "Ur." Pages 288–91 in *The Oxford Encyclopedia of Archaeology in the Near East*. Edited by E. M. Meyers. New York: Oxford University Press, 1997.

Rashkow, Ilona N. *The Phallacy of Genesis: A Feminist-Psychoanalytic Approach*. Louisville: Westminster/John Knox Press, 1993.

Rendsburg, Gary A. *The Redaction of Genesis*. Winona Lake: Eisenbrauns, 1986.

Revell, E. J. "Masorah." *ABD* 4:592–93.

———. "Masoretes." *ABD* 4:593–97.

———. "Masoretic Text." *ABD* 4:597–99.

Robinson, R. B. "Literary Functions of the Genealogies of Genesis." *CBQ* 48 (1986): 601–2.

Roth, Martha T. *Law Collections from Mesopotamia and Asia Minor*. SBL Writings from the Ancient World. Atlanta: Scholars Press, 1995.

Roth, Martha T., A. Leo Oppenheim, Erica Reiner, et al., eds. *The Assyrian Dictionary of the Oriental Institute of the University of Chicago*. Vol. 1: *A, Part 2*. Chicago: Oriental Institute, 1968. Vol. 11: *N, Part 1*. Chicago: Oriental Institute, 1980.

Rulon-Miller, Nina. "Hagar: A Woman with an Attitude." Pages 60–89 in *The World of Genesis: Persons, Places, Perspectives*. Edited by P. R. Davies and D. J. A. Clines. JSOTSup 257. Sheffield: Sheffield Academic Press, 1998.

Schneider, Tammi J. *Judges*. Berit Olam. Collegeville: Liturgical Press, 2000.

Seely, David. "Shur." *ABD* 5:1230.

Speiser, E. A. *Genesis: A New Translation with Introduction and Commentary*. 3d ed. Anchor Bible 1. Garden City, N.Y.: Doubleday, 1985.

Steinberg, Naomi. *Kinship and Marriage in Genesis: A Household Economics Perspective*. Minneapolis: Fortress, 1993.

Teubal, Savina. *Hagar the Egyptian: The Lost Tradition of the Matriarchs*. San Francisco: Harper & Row, 1990.

———. *Sarah the Priestess: The First Matriarch of Genesis*. Athens, Ohio: Ohio University Press, 1984.

Thompson, Henry O. "Hobah." *ABD* 3:235.

Trible, Phyllis. "Genesis 22: The Sacrifice of Sarah." Pages 271–92 in *Women in the Hebrew Bible: A Reader*. Edited by A. Bach. New York: Routledge, 1999.

———. "Hagar: The Desolation of Rejection." Pages 9–36 in *Texts of Terror: Literary-Feminist Readings of Biblical Narratives*. Overtures to Biblical Theology 13. Philadelphia: Fortress, 1984.

Turner, Laurence A. *Announcement of Plot in Genesis*. JSOTSup 96. Sheffield: JSOT Press, 1990.

Vallat, François. "Elam." Translated by Stephen Rosoff. *ABD* 2:424.

Van Dijk-Hemmes, Fokkelien. "Sarai's Exile: A Gender-Motivated Reading of Genesis 12:10–13:2." Pages 222–34 in *A Feminist Companion to Genesis 2*. Edited by A. Brenner. Sheffield: Sheffield Academic Press, 1997.

Von Rad, Gerhard. *Genesis: A Commentary*. The Old Testament Library. Philadelphia: Westminster, 1972.

Westermann, Claus. *Genesis*. Vol. 2: *Genesis 12–36*. Neukirchen-Vluyn: Neukirchener Verlag, 1981.

———. *Genesis 12–36*. Minneapolis: Augsburg, 1985.

———. *Genesis: A Practical Commentary in Text and Interpretation*. Translated by David Green. Grand Rapids: Eerdmans, 1987.

Yee, Gale A. "Sarah." *ABD* 4:981–82.

Yoffee, Norman. "The Economy of Ancient Western Asia." Pages 1387–99 in vol. 3 of *Civilizations of the Ancient Near East*. Edited by J. M. Sasson. New York: Charles Scribner's Sons, 1995.

Zakovitch, Yair. "The Exodus from Ur of Chaldeans: A Chapter in Literary Archaeology." Pages 429–42 in *Ki Baruch Hu [he who is blessed]: Ancient Near Eastern Studies in Honor of Baruch A. Levine*. Edited by R. Chazan, W. W. Hallo, and L. H. Schiffman. Winona Lake: Eisenbrauns, 1999.

Zettler, Richard L., and Lee Horne. *Treasures from the Royal Tombs of Ur*. Philadelphia: University Museum of Archaeology and Anthropology, 1998.

Index

Abel, 10, 21

Abimelech, 16, 26, 34, 39, 73, 85, 88, 90, 102, 105, 108, 116

Adam, 21, 35

Acts, 7:4 — 22

Ai, 30

Amah, 97–98

Ammon/Ammonites, 78, 83

Amos
  2:6 — 34
  8:6 — 34

Arabah, 30, 85

Aram Naharaim, 14, 19, 27, 113, 118

Babel, 9–10, 13, 28

Babylon, 9, 51–52, 64

Balak, 28

Balaam, 28

Barren/Barrenness, 17–18, 28, 30, 33, 62–63, 91, 112, 131–32

Bathsheba, 32, 108

Beauty, 31–32, 34, 86, 108

Beer-lahai-roi, 65, 120

Beer-sheba, 39, 85, 101, 103, 106–7, 111, 114–15

Benjamin, 98

Bethel, 30

Bethuel, 112

Bilhah, 49, 63, 97, 123

Bless/blessing, 27–28, 44, 53, 55–56, 58, 67, 73, 95, 98, 105, 120, 122

Brother, 16, 25, 32, 64, 87, 89, 90, 94, 107, 111–13, 125

Cain, 10, 21, 35

Canaan, 12, 19, 22, 24, 29, 37–38, 44, 48, 60, 64, 84, 98, 117, 125

Canaanites, 17, 27, 38, 118

Chaldees/Chaldeans, 14–15, 19, 25–26

II Chronicles, 7:8 — 62

Circumcision, 56, 57, 59, 61, 67, 91, 92, 98, 100

Concubine, 48, 63, 97, 109, 113, 118–19

Courtiers, 32, 34
Curse/cursing, 28, 50

Damascus, 43
Daughter, 16, 18, 26, 27, 77, 118,
    125
David, 4, 32, 49, 108
Death, 5, 11, 13, 15, 19, 22, 25, 28,
    106, 111, 113–14, 116–17, 119,
    121, 127

Eden, (garden of), 21
Ephron, 116
Egypt, 1, 4, 19, 24–25, 30, 34, 36,
    40, 42, 44–45, 48–49, 54, 62–64,
    73, 83–86, 88–90, 93, 101–2,
    105, 109, 116, 124, 126
Egyptian, 1, 32–33, 35, 44–45, 47,
    50, 54–55, 85–86, 101–2, 108
El Elyon, 44–45
Elam, 43
Eliezer, 45
Elim, 84
Ellasar, 43, 62
Ephron, 116
'Erets, 14
Eshnunna, 64
Esau, 18, 97–98
Eve, 21, 35
Exodus, 4, 31, 35, 39
Exodus
    1   40
    1:11–12   50
    1:12   50
    1:16   32
    1:22   32
    15:22–26   64
    15:22–27   84
    21:17   28, 49
Ezekiel
    16:13   68
    47:19   62
    48:28   62

Faith, 6, 27, 33, 36, 46, 48, 74, 105,
    112, 118, 131–32
Famine, 30, 33, 35–36, 39, 83
Father, 11, 13–16, 19, 22, 25–26, 29,
    56–57, 59, 68, 78–79, 83, 87, 89,
    96–97, 103–4, 106, 112, 119
Fertility, 18, 47, 50, 52, 59, 69, 99
Flood, 13, 21
Foreign, 19, 34, 40, 43–44, 54, 86, 88,
    90, 94–95, 116
Foreshadowing, 4, 10, 27, 29, 32, 35,
    105

Galatians
    4:21–31   132
    4:30   132, 133
Genealogy/genealogies, genealogical,
    8, 11, 13, 18, 20, 89, 125
Genesis
    1–11   8, 125
    2:17   21
    3:13   35
    3:14   28
    3:14–17   21
    3:17   28
    3:23–24   21
    4:1–5   10
    4:10   35
    5   11
    5:6–27   5
    5:32   21
    6:5–8:12   21
    6:8–9   12
    6:9   39
    9:11   10
    9:18   21
    10:1   21
    10:2–12   10
    10:12–20   10
    10:19   38, 84
    10:21–31   10
    11   8, 9, 11, 19, 20,
                        25, 112, 125, 127

Genesis (*continued*)

11:1–9	9, 21
11:4	10, 27–28
11:5–9	10
11:6	10
11:6–8	27
11:8	19
11:10	9, 11
11:24–30	89
11:29–30	89
11:26	22
11:29	112
11:30	112
11:31	18–19, 27
11:10–50:26	12, 18
11:10–32	12
11:26	11–13, 25
11:26–32	13
11:27	11–13
11:28	12–14, 25
11:29	15, 121
11:30–32	9
11:32	8, 14, 22
11–12	125
11–17	5
11–24	4
11:20	62
11:29	17, 121
11:29–30	17
11:30	17
11:31	14, 16, 19, 25–26
11:32	25
12	20, 24–25, 27, 36–37, 42, 45–47, 83, 85, 89, 126
12–13	24
12–36	8
12:1	8, 14–15, 19, 25–26, 44, 56, 60
12:1–9	36, 39, 125
12:1–25:11	12
12:2	10, 27, 56–57, 126
12:3	28, 50
12:4	25, 29, 48

12:4–5	26
12:5	29
12:6	30
12:7	37, 57
12:8	30
12:9	24, 30, 83
12:10	30, 33, 83
12:10–20	36, 39, 42, 82–83, 126–27
12:10–13	125
12:10–13:1	87
12:10–13:18	36, 38
12:11	31, 40, 105, 108
12:11–13	89
12:12	32, 44
12:13	32–34, 40, 47
12:14	31, 108
12:14–15	34, 89
12:15	83, 86, 108
12:16	33–34, 36, 47, 109
12:17	45, 102
12:18	88
12:18–19	35, 89
12:19	32
12:19–20	33, 44
12:20	35
13	24–25, 36–38, 42–43, 125
13–14	46
13–15	43, 108
13:1	35–37, 39
13:1–18	36
13:2	47, 109
13:3	37
13:5	37
13:7	38
13:13	80, 87
13:14	53
13:15	37, 39
13:15–16	57
13:18	83, 103, 115
14	43–45, 61, 87, 126
14–15	42, 46, 126

Genesis (*continued*)

14–17	42, 61
14:1	43
14:10	45
14:11–12	43
14:12–16	77
14:13	115
14:14–24	116
14:15	43
14:16	43
14:18	44
14:19	44
14:20	44–45
14:21	44–45
14:22	45
14:23	45
14:24	45
15	42, 45, 48, 57, 126
15:1	45
15:2	45
15:3	105
15:4	45, 48
15:5	46, 55
15:6	6, 27, 46
15:7	39
15:8	46
15:15	57
15:17	44
15:20	46
16	28, 42, 46, 56–57, 95–96, 125–26
16:1	47, 62, 97, 101
16:1–6	46
16:2	40, 47–48, 55
16:3	48–49, 55, 96, 97
16:4	49, 94
16:5	50, 73, 105
16:6	54, 96
16:7	85
16:7–16	53
16:8	54–55
16:9	55
16:10	55, 100–1
16:10–11	99
16:11–12	55, 57
16:14	55, 119
16:15–16	100
16:15	98
16:16	48, 56, 100
17	16, 42, 56–57, 60–61, 67–68, 71, 100, 119, 126, 127
17:1	56
17:2	56
17:4	56
17:4–17	57
17:5	56
17:7	56
17:8	56
17:10	56
17:12	56
17:15–16	59
17:15–21	61, 76
17:16	57–58, 68, 90–91, 95, 99
17:17	58, 70, 72–73, 88, 105, 114
17:18	59, 73, 98, 103
17:19	58–59, 99, 104, 106
17:20	59, 99, 101
17:20–21	95
17:21	59, 67, 83, 90, 91, 95, 99, 102, 104, 106, 114
17:22	59, 99
17:23	60, 98, 100
17:24	67, 100
17:25	98
17:25–26	98
18	56, 60, 66–67, 71, 74–77, 79, 82–83, 87–88, 91, 126
18–19	66
18:1	83, 103, 115
18:1–5	67
18:1–15	66–67, 74, 76, 126
18:2	67
18:3	67

Genesis (*continued*)

18:4	67
18:5	67
18:6	73
18:7	68
18:8	68
18:9	68, 72
18:10	68, 90–91
18:11	69
18:12	69, 72, 92, 132
18:12–15	88
18:13	69, 70, 72–73
18:14	69, 72, 83, 90
18:15	70, 72–73, 76, 126
18:16	74–75, 80
18:16–32	74
18:16–33	66, 74, 76
18:16–19:38	74
18:19	75
18:20	89
18:21	75
18:22	74–76
18:23	75
18:24	75
18:27	40
18:32	75, 104
18:33	75
19	66, 68, 71, 76, 79, 82, 87, 115, 126
19:1	74
19:3	77
19:4	77
19:5	77
19:6–8	77
19:9	77
19:10	77
19:11	77
19:12	77
19:13–14	77
19:15	74, 77
19:15–16	77
19:17	77
19:20	77

19:21	77
19:22	77
19:23	81
19:24	78
19:25	78
19:26	78
19:28	78
19:29	74–75, 78
19:30	78, 81
19:31	78, 81
19:33–35	78
19:37–38	78, 83
20	39, 73, 76, 79, 82–84, 87–88, 100, 107, 126
20–22	82–83
20:1	64, 83–85, 115
20:2	84–86, 89, 105
20:3	87
20:3–4	90
20:4	87
20:5	87
20:6	102
20:7	88, 90
20:8	88
20:9	88, 90
20:10	88
20:11	88–89, 105
20:12	16, 26, 89
20:13	89
20:14	90–91
20:14–18	116
20:15	90, 101
20:16	90
20:17	90–91
20:17–18	90
21	39, 84, 93, 100, 103, 106–7, 114, 127, 133
21:1	73, 91–92, 102
21:2	83, 92, 100, 112
21:3	92
21:4	92
21:5	22, 67, 92, 114
21:6	88, 92, 106, 121

Genesis (*continued*)

21:7   92
21:8   93, 100
21:9   93
21:9–21   104
21:10   63, 93, 97, 99, 101,
                   106, 121, 132
21:11   9, 104
21:12   63, 99, 102, 106, 133
21:12–14   99
21:13   99
21:14   27, 100–1, 104
21:15–16   101
21:16–17   101
21:17   101–2
21:19   101
21:20   101
21:20–21   101
21:21   39, 85, 103
21:22   102
21:22–24   39
21:22–34   102, 116
21:34   103
22   73, 99, 102–4, 106–7,
      111, 114–15, 118, 121, 127
22:1   103, 111
22:2   27, 99–100, 104, 119
22:3–4   104
22:5–6   104
22:6–8   103
22:7   104
22:7–8   104
22:8   104
22:9–10   104
22:11   27
22:11–12   104
22:12   105
22:13   105
22:14   105
22:15–18   105
22:17–18   106
22:19   39, 106–7, 114
22:20   112–13

22:20–22   17
22:20–24   107, 111, 121
22:21   112–13
22:22   112–13
22:22–23   12
22:23   112
22:24   107, 113
23   107, 111, 113, 117, 121
23:1   113–14
23:2   107, 115–16, 119, 122
23:4   44, 116
23:5–18   116
23:15–16   116
24   26, 106, 112
24:1   119, 122
24:2   118
24:2–4   120
24:3   17
24:3–4   118
24:4   27, 118
24:6   118
24:7   118, 120
24:10   14, 19, 27
24:12–14   120
24:15–27   120
24:24   14
24:27   120
24:36   122
24:40   118
24:62   84, 119–20
24:66   120
24:67   17, 106, 114, 120–21
25:1   118
25:1–10   119
25:2   118
25:5   119, 122
25:5–6   118
25:6   119
25:7   114
25:8   119
25:9   103, 119
25:11   119, 122
25:12   100, 103

Genesis (*continued*)
25:12–18   57
25:12–26   12
25:16   64
25:17   114
25:18–19   123
25:20   19, 114
25:21   91
25:26   119
25:27–35:29   12
26   84
26:1–11   82
29:24   47, 49, 97
29:29   47, 49, 97
30:1–12   47
30:3–13   49
30:3   97
30:4   97
30:7   97
30:9   97
30:10   97
31:33   63, 98
33:1–2   98
33:2   97
35:22–26   98
35:22   97
35:25   97
35:26   97
35:27   115, 118
36:1–43   12
37:2   97
37:2–50:26   98
47:29   122
49   98
Ger, 31, 33, 116
Gerar, 26, 34, 64, 76, 78–79, 82–86, 88, 105, 126
Goiim, 43
Gomorrah, 44, 66–67, 71, 74–76, 82, 84, 88–89, 91, 115

Hagar, 1, 4, 22, 39, 42, 46, 48, 51, 53, 56, 61, 64, 73, 84, 85, 93–

103, 106–7, 119, 124, 125, 131–32
Ham, 10, 21
Hammurabi of Babylon, 51–52, 64, 96–97, 109
Haran (person), 13–16, 18, 25, 112
Haran (place), 14, 16, 19, 22, 25, 27, 30, 63, 118
Harem, 38, 45, 73
Havilah, 64
Hebrews
11:8   27
11:11   132
Hebron, 83, 85, 103, 114–15, 117, 122
Heir, 11–12, 16, 18, 29, 38, 45–46, 56–57, 59–60, 67, 94, 97–99, 118, 127
Hittites, 32, 62, 116–17
Hobah, 43
Husband, 32, 42, 48, 51–53, 69, 73, 79, 87, 94–95, 121, 127, 132

Iscah, 15–16, 112
'ishah, 34, 98
Isaiah, 51:2   122
Israel, 1, 9, 13, 15, 28, 32, 54, 62, 64, 78

Jacob, 18, 29, 31, 47, 63, 97–98, 120
Japheth, 10, 21
Jerusalem, 44
Joseph, 31, 39, 97–98, 129
Joshua
14:15   122
15:4   62
15:23   84
15:47   62
24:2   26
24:3   26
24:2–3   19
Joy, 59, 69–72, 92–93, 121, 132
Judah, 15, 30, 62, 84

Judges
  1:10 — 122
  4–5 — 62
  6–9 — 62
  11 — 62
  12:1–6 — 21
  13–16 — 62

Kadesh, 64, 84–85, 101
Keturah, 118–19
I Kings
  2:8 — 49
  4:22 — 68
  8:65 — 62
  20:31 — 40
  22:13 — 40
Kiriath-arba, 114–15, 122

Laban, 29, 63
Lamech, 21
Laugh/laughter, 58, 60, 69, 72–73, 79, 88–89, 92, 106
Law, 40, 51–52, 63–64, 97
Law codes, 51, 64, 95, 109, 126
Leah, 49, 63, 97–98
Leviticus, 19:14 — 28
Lipit-Ishtar, 64, 95–97
Lot, 3, 4, 12–13, 15–16, 18, 22, 24, 26, 29, 35, 38, 42, 46, 61, 74, 76, 80, 83, 115, 125–26
Lot's daughters, 78–80, 83
Lot's wife, 77–78
LXX, 13, 22, 93, 114

II Maccabees, 7:27 — 93
Machpelah, 103, 115, 117, 119–20
Maid/handmaid, 47, 49, 55, 63, 98
Mamre, 67, 83, 85, 114–15, 117, 122
Marah, 64, 84
Marriage, 16, 34, 86, 90, 119
Masorah, 2
Masoretes, 2, 11, 12, 24, 30, 42, 56–57, 66, 74, 76, 84, 91, 107

Masoretic, 3, 66, 74, 84, 124, 126
Matriarch, 18, 27, 113, 122
Melchizedek, 44–45
Menopause, 69
Mesopotamia, 9, 14, 15, 40, 51–52, 60, 62, 64, 95, 105
Messenger (angel), 53, 55, 66–69, 71, 72, 74–77, 79, 91, 115, 118
Midrash, 26
Milcah, 15–17, 89, 112–13, 127
Moab/Moabites, 78, 83
Moreh, 30
Moriah, 27, 119

Na', 31, 33, 40, 47
Naditu, 52, 64
Nahor (person), 12–13, 16, 18–19, 27, 89, 107, 111–13, 125
Nahor (city), 14, 27, 107
Name/names/naming, 3–4, 9, 18, 21, 27–28, 55, 60, 67, 92, 95, 100, 113, 120, 125
Narrator, 12, 17, 30, 35, 39, 49, 53, 59, 69, 71, 74–75, 78, 86–87, 89, 92, 100, 102, 104, 108, 114, 119–20, 125
Negev, 30, 36, 64, 82–83, 85, 114–16, 120
New Testament, 6, 54, 64, 124, 128, 130–32
Noah, 10, 13, 21, 26, 38–39
Numbers
  13:26 — 85
  22:6 — 28
  22:12 — 28
  34:5 — 62
Nuzi, 32, 116

Paran, 85, 101
Parashah, 24, 39, 56, 60–61, 113
Patriarchy, Patriarchal, 4, 17, 95, 114, 124
Paul, 131–32

Perizzites, 38
I Peter, 3:6   132
Pharaoh, 32, 34–35, 38, 44–45, 49,
    63, 73, 83, 86–89
Pilegesh, 97, 113, 122
Plagues, 35
Play/playing, 93–94
Pray, 91
Pregnancy/Pregnant, 50–51, 73, 91,
    119
Primeval History, 8–9, 129
Prophet, 90–91
Proverbs, 30:21–23   53
Psalms, 76:2   44

Qalal, 28, 49, 50

Rabshakeh, 21
Rachel, 49, 63, 97–98, 123
Rebekah, 12, 17, 19, 27, 91, 106,
    112–15, 118, 120–22
Reuben, 97
Romans
    4:1–3   6
    4:19   131

Sacrifice, 10, 27, 46, 79, 91, 102–3,
    105–6, 111–12, 115, 117, 121,
    127
Salem, 44
I Samuel
    1:23   93
    25:1   116
II Samuel
    6:23   23
    11:4   108
    11   32
    18:18   44
Septuagint. *See* LXX
Serpent, 21, 28
Servant, 14, 27, 42, 68, 111, 118,
    120

Seth, 13, 39
Sexual/sexually, 34, 69, 71, 78–79,
    86–88, 90, 94, 108, 132
Shechem, 30
Shem, 9–11, 13, 18–21, 26
Shifkhah, 47, 97–98
Shinar, 43, 62
Shur, 54, 64, 84–85
Sinai, 84
Sister, 16, 33, 35, 86–90
Slave, 1, 47, 51–55, 64, 90–91, 93–
    98, 101
Slavery, 40, 52, 54–55, 132–33
Snake. *See* Serpent
Sodom, 43, 46, 66–67, 71, 74–80,
    82, 84, 87–89, 91, 115, 126
Sojourn, 24, 30, 31, 48, 56
Song of Songs, 1:15–16   31

Tent/s, 30, 63, 67, 68, 71, 77, 98,
    120, 122
Terah, 9, 12–14, 18–20, 22, 25, 27,
    29, 89, 119, 125
Test, 71, 73, 82, 86, 99, 102–3, 105–
    7, 117–18, 121, 127, 129
Theology, theological, 4, 36, 48, 74,
    76, 87, 106, 125, 131
Tithe/tithing, 44–45
Tower, 9–10, 27
Tower of Babel, 10, 19–21, 27, 45,
    125
Transjordan, 43

Ur, 14, 16, 18–19, 22, 25–27, 118
Ur Nammu, 53, 64
Uriah, 32

Wealth, 33, 36, 38, 43, 90, 108–9
Wife-sister, 32, 36, 82–83, 101

Zilpah, 49, 63, 97, 113
Zoar, 78, 81